The Magic of Cooking with Really Good Broth

Johnny Prep

With Chef Kelli Lewton

First Printing, 2013
ISBN 978-0-9889916-0-6
Printed in Korea

JP Culinary Entertainment, LLC 855 Harsdale Rd., Bloomfield Hills, MI 48302
www.johnnyprep.com

Contents

Johnny Prep's Series: Culinary School for the Home Cook

I love to eat good food. I always have.

Throughout my life and career, this absolute love for eating has driven my passion for cooking. I'm fortunate to have been exposed to several amazing cooks and chefs from whom I've learned and developed my style. My first mentor was my mother—one of the few women I know who can stretch phyllo dough by hand! She could cook circles around most chefs. As a first-generation immigrant, she prepared Croatian-style meals daily with an aim for perfectionism and a deep sense of authenticity. That attention to exactness is a mindset that she handed down to me through my genes, and it's both a blessing and a curse.

Following her on my list of mentors and teachers are Chef Paul Prudhomme, Chef Takashi Yagihashi, Chef Milos Chihelka, Chef Ed Janos, Chef Glenn Cockburn, Chef Brian Polcyn, Chef Joseph Decker, Chef Jeffrey Gabriel, Chef Kelli Lewton, and Chef Marcus Haight. Every time I had the opportunity to learn from someone else, I approached it with my mother's perfectionism. I was called "focused" and "intense." Now comes the curse of perfectionism. . .

My formal cooking education has been kind of backwards. I started taking continuing education classes from Certified Master Chefs (CMC) before I had my base formal culinary education. In fact, I had amassed over 30,000 hours of practice at my craft before I attended my first full day of culinary school. My department chair summarized it best when he said, "You're going to walk into some classes and learn a lot; others probably not so much."

It was true. I had never attempted to do much baking or pastry work through the years. This had a lot to do with my mom's European background and the prevalence of nuts in her desserts. I'm allergic to most nuts and rarely was able to eat many of the traditional nut rolls and strudels she would create, so my fondness for baked goods never developed. Learning from one of only three American-born certified master pastry chefs in the country was indeed an eye-opening learning experience. In the classes that focused on first courses, main courses, and appetizers, on the other hand, I already knew much of what they were teaching. I had more than one chef ask why I was even going through all the effort.

I like to compare it to watching *The Sixth Sense*. The film is famous for having an unexpected ending. When the credits roll you inevitably say, "I didn't see that coming!" But when you watch the movie a second time, you see all of the little hints you missed the first time and you say, "Oh yeah. . ." That's what cooking school has been like for me. I've seen and practiced the vast majority of the techniques many times. But it's those little tips and tricks that you pick up from the chefs along the way that enrich and refine your skills and education and make the experience so rewarding and enjoyable.

It was also interesting to go through chef's school at the same time I was working with the local schools in Bloomfield Hills, Michigan, where I live and was doing professional development with teachers. I spend quite a bit of my time working with educators teaching the science of quality. Through the course of my work I've noticed the anxiety and stress that the academic community feels to raise standardized test scores, especially versus international competition. It's a unique and uncomfortable position for U.S. citizens not to be no. 1 in the developed world for education, let alone no. 17 (per a 2012 global report by education firm Pearson). Naturally, educators everywhere are looking for solutions.

One area of education that has changed dramatically over the years is the availability of content. It wasn't that long ago when people went to schools and libraries for academic knowledge. But today, information is available in many formats, and schools are one of many, many sources available. The key is to find the format that works best for your learning style and is most convenient to your lifestyle. This is wake-up call for many educators. Instead of merely lecturing content day-in-and-day-out, they have to provide additional value through coaching, motivation, and experiential learning exercises. If all they do is provide content, they are on the train to obsolescence.

Now let's apply that line of thinking to the world of culinary education. Cooking schools are where people go to obtain the greatest access to a wide variety of professional certified chef instructors and to learn classical technique. These schools are entrenched in the traditions of Auguste Escoffier, who was the father of modern cooking. He developed the basic organizational structure that most restaurants have either implemented or adapted. Remember Julia Child's story of how she cooked every recipe in the Escoffier cookbook? He was also the co-founder of the Ritz Carlton Hotel along with Steve Carlton. Escoffier was the first to really define how restaurant quality food should be prepared and how the restaurants themselves should be organized to provide that food. In other words, he was all about restaurants.

And so are the vast majority of culinary schools

today. The cooking school that I attended is a formal school that has one of the highest percentages of Certified Master Chefs in the country. (That's the highest certification a chef can achieve in the internationally recognized certifying body). They believe deeply, as do most schools, that they should teach classical technique. They give you the opportunity to see it taught by different instructors. Each bring their own interpretations and styles. Then you, the graduate, can begin your professional career and apply the similarities and differences of these styles in the way you see fit. It's very clear; you're there to be trained for a career. They don't even joke about the fact that they aren't interested in students who just want to learn how to be better home cooks.

They don't feel that much more comfortable with people who are engaged in food media, like me. The vast majority of these instructors don't pay attention to e-books, food television, websites, blogs, videos, and mobile apps. Most have been so involved in the totally energy-monopolizing industry of restaurants that they simply don't have the time—they view it as a distraction from their craft. It's amazing to me how many incredibly talented chefs haven't even been inclined to complete a cookbook.

Of course some of this is just an extension of their business sense. First, they don't want others cooking their recipes. They want those people to come to their restaurants. Second, most chefs look down on home cooks. How many times have I heard that just because

all your friends tell you that you make the best meatloaf ever, that doesn't qualify you for culinary school? While that may sound offensive, I think it's just the nature of the industry. To be a successful chef you have to be disciplined, creative, somewhat controlling and impeccably skilled with a refined palate and reasonably good business sense. When you accumulate those kind of attributes it can lead to an inflated ego. Chef Marcus Height lectured in my class that the three most common downfalls of a great chef are alcohol, drugs, and ego. Unfortunately, it's the presence of the ego that has closed many chefs off to the need for innovative and accessible culinary education for the home cook.

An incredible thirst for culinary education exists in this country. Food media has grown dramatically over the last decade, and along with that a heightened interest in cooking. Everyone—even kids—are becoming engaged as home cooks, and they're getting better at it, but they still want to learn some technique.

I have been on the forefront of this movement for many years. Beyond my professional and personal experience, I have been highly active as a cooking teacher. I have done this in schools. I have formed clubs. I have structured catering events as classes. Basically, I really like to coach and teach. I'm also a big fan of educational tools such as multi-media and digital formats and platforms.

With this in mind, I have established a goal to bridge the gap of classical culinary training with the needs of the home cook. To accomplish this, I'm creating a series of digitally and conventionally formatted media to allow the home cook easy access to entertaining instruction on classical culinary techniques that can be applied to preparing easy, nutritious, and contemporary foods. This series takes the parts of culinary school that are pertinent to home cooks and gives the same comprehensive instruction as a full culinary degree—with some minor upgrades tailored to the home cook. For instance, we dropped the class on dining room management. We added much more emphasis on nutrition and cooking for and with kids. We talk about purchasing products in a retail environment. We also provide tips that help minimize kitchen clean-up (not something most chefs even contemplate).

So welcome to *Johnny Prep's Series: Culinary School for the Home Cook*. This first cookbook, *The Magic of Cooking With Really Good Broth* and the associated videos, focus on the first thing you learn in a cooking class at culinary school, broths and stocks.

Introduction

Most home cooks don't know that restaurant chefs have two "tools" in their bag of tricks that they rely on to enhance the succulent flavor of dishes—good quality broths and stocks. Chefs use them liberally because it provides a complexity and depth of flavor that make meals stand out. You simply cannot make an exquisite sauce without them! Although it does make me chuckle when I hear TV chefs dispense recipe and restaurant secrets. When preparing a dish, they casually take out a container of deeply flavored stock that was made in-house at the restaurant. They neglect to share the fact that you, the home cook, can have access to this kind of ingredient.

Yes, you too can make this yourself and should be using it in many of your favorite recipes. So I've decided to bust that secret wide open and get the entire home cooking world plugged into the value and power that stocks and broths add to your meals.

After years of constantly pursuing convenience, convenience, and more convenience, we are starting to wake up to the fact that we have sacrificed dearly for our obsession with quick and readily available meals.

Quality, flavor, and nutrition have become outsourced and marginalized and our mouths and our bodies are feeling the repercussions of that culture of food. But with a little time and attention, home cooks can reverse that trend by creating rich-tasting, high quality broth- and stock-based dishes that rival the best chefs and eateries.

Flavor and convenience are odd bedfellows. Inherently, convenience implies "quick" and "easy-to-do." Yet deriving the sumptuous, elegant flavors that so many ingredients have to offer is rarely quick and not often that easy for the home cook. In today's world, not many people are willing to commit hours of time to preparing a meal from scratch, from a recipe. But is it really the time required, or is it just a lack of some good old-fashioned planning and know-how that's missing?

You don't need to be trained at the finest culinary school or plan out your meals in detail or way in advance to be a good cook—common sense should dictate how much time you spend on preparing a meal. While you are doing "other stuff," you can be multi-tasking, making your own stock- or a broth-based dish. Finding a few minutes to check a simmering pot while watching the tube or cleaning up your living room isn't too hard.

The time you spend preparing your own stocks and broths is worth it, because once you're done, you can freeze your luscious liquid flavorizors in small ice cube packages for quick taste enhancers. Or freeze pre-measured amounts that match what you'll need for your favorite recipes, like gumbos, soups, or sauces. But whatever you do, incorporate the flavors of stocks and broths in everything you can, because they just make meals better.

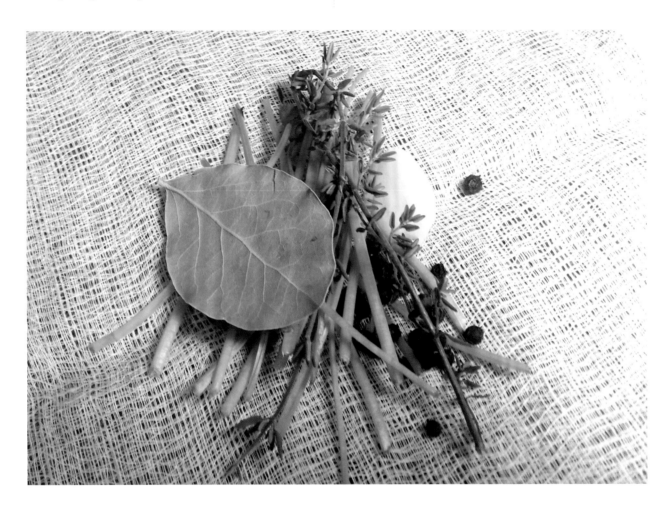

About Broth and Stock

Historically, the word "broth" means "something that has been brewed"; or in other words, something that has been boiled. It wasn't until the 17th century that that "something" became predominantly meat. And meat is a key word. It separates what is commonly known as stock from broth. Stock is made from bones while broth is made from meat. Of course this definition can get blurry. Classical kitchens that use significant amounts of stock purchase chicken feet and backs to make the stock. Both the feet and the backs have some meat attached to their bones.

Likewise, broths most commonly are made from whole pieces of meat that are "on the bone." So both stocks and broths typically have bones and meat in them. The difference between the two is a matter of ratio. Stocks have a higher ratio of bone and broths have a higher ratio of meat—and you definitely want both because they each make an important contribution to taste and flavor.

The meat in broth is what gives it a richer, more intense flavor than stocks. Broths are designed to be served as stand-alone items or dressed up with some garnishes. Stocks, on the other hand, are meant to be incorporated into other items such as sauces or braising liquids to add and enhance flavor. The logical extension of this is that broths can be used in place of stocks, and the only side effect is you get more flavor. (I can live with that.) Stocks, however, aren't something I want to place in a bowl in front of a guest by itself because the flavor would be too skimpy. So in keeping with the economical nature of a home kitchen, choosing to have broth on hand for uses in both applications is the more common sense approach.

The contributions that meat, bones, vegetables, and shells make to liquids are similar but also unique in certain ways. Meat is the muscle of an animal and is meant to be eaten. Meat generates both its rich color and flavor from active use of the muscle. So while inactive muscles create tender meats, the flavor lacks. Conversely, meat that comes from active muscles, such as the shoulder or calves, is generally tough and has a lot of connective tissue, but it has a lot of flavor! These are the cuts that are best used for broths. While making these broths the connective tissues in the meats will break down and tenderize the meat. This then makes the afterlife of meat used for a broth an excellent candidate for such things as chicken salad, taco meat, pastas, ravioli fillings and much more.

Bones on the other hand give the broth body. The collagen in the bones converts to gelatin as the broth is heated. Gelatin infuses the broth with a thicker consistency and a more enjoyable mouth feel. It also makes your soups more filling even in absence of fat! Evidence also reveals that the bones contribute glucosamine and chondroitin to the broth, a common supplement that helps reduce joint pain.

As a home cook, you certainly don't want to live within these definitions of stocks and broths alone. Bones and meat are surely the star players in these savory liquids, but they have a strong supporting staff. Aromatics and herbs play a role as well. Broths, like most foods, have a complex layering of flavors. You want to integrate as many complimentary flavors as you can to provide a luxurious complexity to your dishes. This is where home cooks can really start to play on the same field as chefs. In classical technique, a sachet or bouquet garni along with mirepoix is frequently added to broths to create this complexity. Each of these are a different combination of root vegetables, herbs, and spices. As you will see, their ingredients are included in most of our broth recipes. But all of these combinations are open to editorial discretion, and the creative home cook will be rewarded by adding and subtracting based on their own tastes.

Quite often the sachet and bouquet garni are wrapped up in cheese cloth or a coffee filter both for the purposes of easy removal and so they keep the smaller ingredients from being removed during skimming. To some degree, it really is a matter of whether the ingredients are going to be strained. If the whole pot is going to be strained at some point, don't bother wrapping these little goodies up. It's just a waste of cheesecloth and time.

HERE ARE THE BASE INGREDIENTS FOR THE FRENCH TERMS:

Mirepoix
50% diced onions
25% diced carrots
25% diced celery
Note: parsnips or celery root are often considered

Sachet
thyme sprig
parsley stems
black peppercorns
bay leaf
Note: a garlic clove is commonly added

Bouquet Garni
thyme sprig
parsley stems
bay leaf
leek leaves
section of celery stalk

HERE ARE A FEW OTHER COMBINATIONS OFTEN USED IN CONTEMPORARY TECHNIQUES:

Asian Aromatics
40% ginger
40% garlic
20% green onion

The Trinity (Louisiana Cookery)
50% onion
25% celery
25% green pepper

Matignon (commonly known as an edible Mirepoix and classically used as a garnish)
fine diced ham
fine diced onion
fine diced celery
fine diced carrots
sprig of thyme (removed after cooking)
bay leaf (removed after cooking)

ONION BRÛLÉE
Peel an onion and cut in half across the root end. Then place it cut side down in a lightly oiled pan and cook over medium high heat until the one surface is deeply browned but not burnt.

RICH BROTHS
For the purposes of the home cook, I have combined the concepts of a brown stock and a rich broth. Both are more deeply flavored than regular broths and stocks. These work nicely with dark sauces and braised dishes containing red meats. The key here is that the flavor of the ingredients are developed by browning them prior to adding them to the pot. This includes the bones and the meats.

One of my favorite broths is one that uses a rotisserie chicken to add color and depth of flavor. I typically brown all of my meats before making a broth for additional flavor. Make sure you brown the meat and bones in the same pan as you make the stock so the fond (the brown stuff that sticks to the bottom of the pan) gets into the broth. That adds a lot of taste. Remember, fond is flavor! If you wish to brown the bones in the oven, then deglaze your pan with some stock or some wine and add this to your pot.

Rich broths can also be made by adding a large amount of other vegetables. Onion soup is a good example. Once again, you want to add some color to those onions first by caramelizing them in the pan before adding liquid.

Another technique to add color and flavor to your broth is to sauté your miropoix until the onions are soft and translucent, and then add one or two tablespoons of tomato paste. Then stir and continue to cook until the tomato paste picks up a brown hue and you get some tomato fond in the bottom of the pan. This technique is also called pincé.

CONSOMMÉ

Few things can be served that have the beauty and elegance of a perfectly clear consommé. The clarity provides a faint veil for this enormously flavorful broth. It's the queen of broths—and quite a pampered queen it is. The technique isn't all that complicated; it just requires attention to detail. The garnishes for these soups allow you to explore your artistic side. They're delicious all by themselves or they can be as ornate as the Sistine Chapel if you care to put in the effort.

On your way to making this royal liquid you must build a raft. No, not the kind you jump off of into the lake. A raft is a floating mass that accumulates in your pot and acts as a filter to pull out all the impurities and clarify the soup. But remember, don't rattle your raft. Once it comes together treat it with care and love. Very gently spoon small amounts of broth over it as it cooks. Chop the ingredients finely and use ground meat so they relinquish their flavor with enthusiasm. Don't push it and prod it and never, ever stir it once it forms (or else you have to start over).

The process of making consommé is quite inadequately called a clarification method. But that's only half the story. The ingredients that comprise a raft add enormous amounts of flavor. In this book I give only one recipe for consommé. It happens to be my favorite, a golden consommé. This luscious broth takes chicken broth and adds beef to the raft for a uniquely complex and delicious flavor. Once you see the size of the raft in relation to the broth you'll understand why so much flavor is added. This isn't the queen of broths for nothing. . .

The raft's key ingredient is the egg whites (many cooks also add the shells, but that isn't necessary). You mix egg whites with miropoix, bouquet garni ingredients, and ground meat. Then you start with cold broth or stock. Mix them together well with a large spoon and slowly bring the broth up to about 120 degrees (or until it is too hot to touch) while stirring gently. Then stop stirring and never stir again. When it comes to a simmer, immediately (do not walk away from the pot until this happens) turn the pot down to a lower simmer. You can carefully baste the raft with a small spoon if you wish.

After an hour to an hour and a half, use a ladle to carefully strain your consommé through a cheesecloth-lined fine sieve. Take your ladle and gently push down at the edge of the pot until the liquid just pours over the edge. Continue to do so until you catch most of the liquid. Don't try to get the last drop. You'll end up with particulate that will cloud the soup. This may sound difficult, but truthfully it's like riding a bike. When you do it once, it becomes a simple, repeatable process.

Equipment, Clean-Up and Storage

To prepare broths, I strongly recommend a 12 quart stock pot that's either stainless steel or anodized aluminum. Broth freezes extremely well so it makes sense to make large batches. I also use a 6 quart pot for small batches on occasion.

You will also need a skimmer to remove the debris that floats to the top as the pot comes to a simmer. You can use anything from a large spoon to a small fine sieve. I prefer to use a small flat ladle because it's easier to reach down into the pot with a ladle shape. Ladles can also skim off fat effectively, but strainers skim just as well.

If you're going to be using sachets or a bouquet garni, you'll want to keep cheesecloth on hand along with some butcher's string to tie them up. You're also going to need cheesecloth for straining some broths such as consommé. You can purchase cheesecloth at any grocery store, but if you want high quality cheesecloth that you can actually reuse, order it from a cheese supply store. I order mine from www.cheesemaking. com. There is also a product called butter muslin that you'll find at cheese supply stores. This is actually a fine cheesecloth and a wonderful broth-straining material for refined soups. Remember to dampen the cheesecloth prior to use so it doesn't soak up your broth.

Having an 8 ounce and 4 ounce ladle available provides flexibility. When transferring large amounts, for example when storing broth, the larger ladle will save you time and is easier on your patience. A 4 ounce ladle, on the other hand, is a bit neater when plating or for pouring your broth into a jar for storage.

It's always a good idea to use a burner that has a low or simmer setting. You don't want to ever rapid boil a soup. A gentle simmer coaxes the flavor out of your ingredients without damaging their natural flavors. Look at it as giving your soup ingredients a nice comfortable Jacuzzi! You're not trying to throw them to their death in a boiling vat.

A sharp chef's knife and a large cutting board are the tools of preference for preparing your ingredients.

The large cutting board will allow you to avoid dirtying a lot of plates before your ingredients go in the pot.

You'll want to have a bowl on hand to dump the scum that is skimmed off the top. If you're going to use a strainer as well, pick a bowl with a strainer that rests nicely on top of it to keep your counters clean.

Cleaning soup pots is actually not too horrible of a chore. The toughest part is normally the ring of residue that develops at the top edge of the broth. Having a soft scrubby sponge with an abrasive side usually works well. If you have the misfortune of not watching your high heat and you burn one of the ingredients on the bottom, it's easiest just to soak the pot for a while with some soap or scouring powder in it to soften up the residue.

My favorite storage containers for broth are re-sealable plastic bags. Just make sure you cool the broth to below 110 degrees first so the plastic doesn't react. I prefer the double-zip feature to minimize the risk of leaks. If you're still concerned about leakage you can double-bag them. This method of storage is super space efficient. I also recommend storing them in quantities that match either standard amounts such a 1 or 2 quarts or quantities that are used in some of your favorite recipes. For instance, I always store my seafood broth in 5 cup measures because that's the amount that goes in my gumbo recipe and I use that often. If you're going to reduce your broths into concentrated flavors (commonly referred to as "glace"), consider storing them in ice cube trays. Then you can simply pop one in a sauce for a kick of flavor.

Broth Nutrition

Chicken soup is legendary for its effects on the common cold. In many circles it's affectionately referred to as "Jewish Penicillin." Some data supports this, but it's not extensive. Dr. Stephen Rennard at the University of Nebraska Medical Center conducted some research that showed that chicken soup helped stop the movement of neutrophil. Neutrophil activity has been known to activate the release of mucous, a symptom of colds. The soup slowed that activity and thus the laboratory link to this powerful side bonus. Beyond lab work, there are other logical reasons why chicken soup is perfect for relieving your coughing and sniffling:

Cleansing. Drinking lots of fluids is often advised when you're ill. Often when you're sick, antigens need to be flushed out in order to regain your health. The broth in chicken soup provides this benefit.

Disinfecting. Salt is an integral element to broths and soups when they are served, so when it's consumed it acts in much the same way as gargling warm salt water. It removes bacteria in the throat, mouth, and tonsils.

Clears sinuses. As a warm liquid, it can help to clear the sinuses with steam.

Strengthening. The nutrients from the chicken and vegetables help to rebuild your strength when you're feeling tired or lethargic.

Finding nutritional data on homemade broth is a difficult task. One would think that in this day and age, a quick spin on the Internet would reveal all of the information you need. Most nutritional websites only provide an analysis of canned broths or dried or condensed products that are commercially prepared. Even in the USDA nutritional database, homemade broths aren't listed. But if you keep searching, they do have the data for homemade stocks. When you look at those lists (provided on the next page) you see that stocks are low in calories and have trace amounts of many minerals and vitamins. The biggest negative is sodium content, which is controlled by you, the cook.

When making broth as an ingredient in other dishes, it's in an unseasoned form. When you use broth as the main base for a soup, then you season it directly with salt and pepper. In this case, salt becomes a big part of the nutritional equation, because there are limitations on salt intake that you'll want to consider.

Broth is a flavoring liquid that's used for braising, stewing, and steaming. It's also used in sauces, stuffing and dressings, and to make rice pilafs and risottos, just to name a few. When using broth as an ingredient, it brings many nutritional elements to play.

One of the elements that doesn't show up in nutritional analysis is gelatin. Gelatin in meat broth gives it body. Gelatin comes from collagen, which is one of the materials that make up cartilage and bone. WebMD reports that there is clinical evidence to support the notion that gelatin might relieve pain and improve joint function in patients with osteoarthritis.

Glucosamine and chondroitin are also present in cartilage and bones. These substances have shown in studies to provide relief from joint pain. Broths derive glucosamine and chondroitin from the bones and cartilage. Many holistic doctors and nutritional traditionalists promote the use of broths for their health benefits, but the data available isn't even close to satisfying the requirements of government agencies to make recommendations for those benefits.

Back to the topic of sodium or salt: The recommendations in the 2010 Dietary Guidelines published by the USDA (found at www.cnpp.usda.gov/dietaryguidelines.htm) show an upper limit of salt intake of 2300 mg and an adequate intake of 1500 mg as their recommendations. If you're older, a child, have hypertension or high blood pressure, or if you're African American, it suggests you use the 1500 mg target. The guidelines indicate a direct correlation between blood pressure and sodium intake. Clearly, if you have blood pressure issues, you should understand the dietary effects when deciding how much to salt your broth. When you look at the first sentence under the heading of "Sodium" in the guidelines, it reads: "Sodium is an essential nutrient and is needed by the body in relatively small quantities, provided that substantial sweating does not occur."

It never touches the topic of substantial sweating after that line. If you're an active individual who works out three or four times a week, this report provides no information on how to adjust your salt intake. I know all about the uses of salt from my athletic days back in college. They would give us salt pills during two-a-days to keep us from getting dehydrated, so I understand that salt requirements increase with heavy athletic or physical activity.

It also states that only 15 percent of the U.S. population meets their current guidelines, yet 85 percent of the U.S. population doesn't have hypertension. So this recommendation really needs some clarity if it's going to be used by the whole population as a guideline. But blood pressure seems to be the only concern the USDA states with intake, so I plan on using common sense moderation until I see a rise in my blood pressure.

This is by no means a recommendation. You should follow the guidance of a licensed health care provider for your individual needs. I just wish the USDA would do a better job in this area. I can tell you that I have had both my doctor and a licensed nutritionist say that the recommendations in this area are unrealistic.

NUTRIENT	UNIT	CHICKEN STOCK VALUE PER 100.0G	1 CUP 240G	UNIT	BEEF STOCK VALUE PER 100.0G	1 CUP 240G	UNIT	FISH STOCK VALUE PER 100.0G	1 CUP 240G
PROXIMATES									
Water	g	92.15	221.16	g	95.89	230.14	g	96.96	225.92
Energy	kcal	36	86	kcal	13	31	kcal	17	40
Protein	g	2.52	6.05	g	1.97	4.73	g	2.26	5.27
Total lipid (fat)	g	1.20	2.88	g	0.09	0.22	g	0.81	1.89
Carbohydrate, by difference	g	3.53	8.47	g	1.20	2.88	g	0.00	0.00
Fiber, total dietary	g	0.0	0.0	g	0.0	0.0	g	0.0	0.0
Sugars, total	g	1.58	3.79	g	0.54	1.30	g	0.00	0.00
MINERALS									
Calcium, Ca	mg	3	7	mg	8	19	mg	3	7
Iron, Fe	mg	0.21	0.50	mg	0.27	0.65	mg	0.01	0.02
Magnesium, Mg	mg	4	10	mg	7	17	mg	7	16
Phosphorus, P	mg	27	65	mg	31	74	mg	56	130
Potassium, K	mg	105	252	mg	185	444	mg	144	336
Sodium, Na	mg	143	343	mg	198	475	mg	156	363
Zinc, Zn	mg	0.14	0.34	mg	0.17	0.41	mg	0.06	0.14
VITAMINS									
Vitamin C, total ascorbic acid	mg	0.2	0.5	mg	0.0	0.0	mg	0.1	0.2
Thiamin	mg	0.035	0.084	mg	0.033	0.079	mg	0.033	0.077
Riboflavin	mg	0.085	0.204	mg	0.091	0.218	mg	0.076	0.177
Niacin	mg	1.584	3.802	mg	0.872	2.093	mg	1.186	2.763
Vitamin B-6	mg	0.061	0.146	mg	0.055	0.132	mg	0.037	0.086
Folate, DFE	µg	5	12	µg	2	5	µg	2	5
Vitamin B-12	µg	0.00	0.00	µg	0.00	0.00	µg	0.69	1.61
Vitamin A, RAE	µg	1	2	µg	0	0	µg	2	5
Vitamin A, IU	IU	3	7	IU	0	0	IU	6	14
Vitamin E (alpha-tocopherol)	mg	0.03	0.07	mg	0.01	0.02	mg	0.17	0.40
Vitamin D (D2 + D3)	µg	0.0	0.0	µg	0.0	0.0	µg	0.0	0.0
Vitamin D	IU	0	0	IU	0	0	IU	0	0
Vitamin K (phylloquinone)	µg	0.2	0.5	µg	0.1	0.2	µg	0.0	0.0
LIPIDS									
Fatty acids, total saturated	g	0.321	0.770	g	0.035	0.084	g	0.203	0.473
Fatty acids, total monounsaturated	g	0.582	1.397	g	0.043	0.103	g	0.236	0.550
Fatty acids, total polyunsaturated	g	0.213	0.511	g	0.005	0.012	g	0.138	0.322
Cholesterol	mg	3	7	mg	0	0	mg	1	2
OTHER									
Caffeine	mg	0	0	mg	0	0	mg	0	0

Mise-en-place

I was first introduced to the term "mise-en-place" by Chef Milos Chehelka, CMC at a cooking class I took many years ago. He explained that it meant "everything in its place," and sure enough his cooking lessons were highly organized. His ingredients were all pre-measured and within easy reach, and his work station was equipped with the tools he needed right at hand. This preparation and his arrangement of his work space clearly made his job easier, so I've been encouraging the use of mise-en-place ever since then.

But it wasn't until my journey through culinary school that I gained a full appreciation for what mise-en-place does for you as a cook. At the end of each culinary course, we would have final exams. But these exams were always done in at least two parts. The first part was a written test following the tradition of most final exams you have in school. But the second part was a practical exam where you had to prepare some foods for examination and grading by the chef instructor. These practical exams typically lasted between two and four hours and they were timed. You were docked points if you didn't get it completed by the specified time. This

was the first instance that I was challenged to work under the clock to that level.

As part of the practical exam, you had to hand in a report on your mise-en-place. In most cases you drew cards to determine what you were to supposed to prepare a few days ahead, so you had time for thorough preparation. That report had to include a shopping list, an equipment list, a timeline, an illustration of your plating, and of course the recipes you were going to use. To do a good job, that report usually took about two hours, especially if you wanted the format and presentation to impress. (Every point helps.)

Now, spending that much time merely preparing to cook—again, three or four hours total—probably sounds excessive. But I can't express how much that preparation helped later on. A practical exam is kind of like cooking a multiple course holiday meal, except the time frames are rigid. You have a lot of different items to prepare and they all have to come together right at the same moment so they are delicious, well-prepared, beautiful, and the proper temperature. Yep, just like Thanksgiving dinner! But the stress is just a touch higher because you have a certified chef dissecting everything you do and picking on the smallest of details. You can't even give them a glass of vino to loosen them up like you can during a holiday meal...

Stress management is one of the greatest advantages of mise-en-place. When you cook something for the first time or prepare a meal for a large group of people or some VIP's (like your in-laws), it's going to be a more (in)tense experience. Mise-en-place helps you relax and perform better. You know that you have everything you need. You know where everything is. You know the order you're going to have to make things. And most importantly, you have made everything you can ahead of time. This is incredibly important because when you're completing your dishes you really want to focus on proper "doneness" and preparation. If you're busy just trying to figure out what you're going to do next, there's no way you're going to give those details there due attention.

The most important factor in creating your mise-en-place is selecting your menu items. This will completely dictate your timing as well as the balance of flavors in the meal. In culinary school you don't often get to dictate your menu but at home you have the flexibility. Take advantage of that and make it work for you. The last thing you want to do is have all your menu items be "a la minute," which means "prepared to order" at the last minute. For instance, mashing your potatoes, making your gravy, and mixing your salad dressing all at the same time would naturally be difficult for just one person to handle at once. And if you are browning off your garlic bread simultaneously, most likely the bread is going to burn! If you choose two dishes that both have last minute pan sauces, good luck.

Don't do this to yourself. At least half of your menu items should be "do-ahead" dishes, which will help minimize the last minute rush.

Try your best to get your shopping done at least two days in advance. That isn't always the right approach for every item, such as fresh bread. But it allows you to do everything you can do the day or night before. It also gives you time to be choosey on where you shop so you find the best quality ingredients possible. Selecting the right stores to shop for the right ingredients is in fact part of your mise-en-place and has a great effect on the quality (and the cost) of your meal.

Nobody likes surprises when preparing meals, but they happen all the time. The pilot won't light. Your can opener breaks. The staple you thought you had was used up by somebody else. Your hot peppers are a lot hotter than you thought. You accidentally over-salt your dish. These surprises all increase the stress of the whole activity. If you're trying to deal with these unexpected events while figuring out what to do next, you're going to overload your brain circuits. Having everything laid out and right at your fingertips allows you to focus on the issue at hand and resolve it, even if that means calling a friend for advice or jumping on the Internet. The crisis management becomes a lot easier if everything else is in cruise control.

You don't have to spend hours preparing. Take a pad and paper and write down your menu. Think through it strategically. Scribble out a task list for two days prior, one day prior, and then for the day of the event. Then break it into morning, afternoon, and a couple of hours before. Take the menu and pull your recipes. You can even cut and paste the ingredients into a shopping list. (Scanners work great for this if the recipes are in a book.) Then jot down any equipment you'll need for a dish if it isn't already located right by the counter where you work. Remember to have on hand a scrap bowl as part of your equipment. Make sure you have ancillary items such as parchment paper and not-stick spray. Double-check your staples such as salt, pepper, flour, sugar, milk and so on.

All of this activity is going to pay off. It will make your meals turn out better and you will be a better cook. Most importantly, you will find that mise-en-place makes cooking a lot more fun!

Cooking With Kids

When I was growing up, the kitchen in our house was pretty much our family room. It was our natural gathering place. I remember lying on the carpeted floor during the winter months so I could keep my feet toasty by the heating vents. My mom was a fantastic cook and she took great joy in feeding me. Since I was her youngest and her only son, I probably received a little extra attention, particularly when it came to food. Truthfully, I was a bit of a bottomless pit. I was tall and skinny and could eat anything I wanted without gaining weight.

I'll never forget being in fifth grade and having a real affinity for sunny side up eggs. It took me every bit of two bites to eat each egg. My mom and I would have a competition. She would see how many eggs she could cook in one pan without breaking a yolk and I would see if I could eat them all. At one point we were up to a dozen eggs a day! Then I started to get stomach aches in the afternoon, so my mom took me to the doctor, who asked what I was eating. I told him about the dozen eggs a morning. He chuckled and told me to cut it back to half a dozen and I should be fine.

I remember watching my mom cook all the time.

Since I was hanging out in the kitchen anyway it was almost impossible not to learn from her. Mom was talkative and would constantly describe what she was doing. I was getting cooking lessons and I didn't even know it.

The first meals I remember preparing were soups. Back then Campbell's tomato soup with a grilled cheese sandwich was a favorite. Although mom always prepared for me at least four meals (that's right—four) a day, I found sneaking in an extra snack or two was a pleasant diversion. I was also a big fan of Mrs. Grass's chicken noodle soup. That little seasoning egg that came in the package was kind of mysterious and fun. Whenever I had a cold or didn't feel well, I would supplement my mom's homemade deliciousness with a little extra bowl that I made myself. . . .Okay, maybe a bit of a bottomless pit was an understatement. Mom used to kid me that I had hollow legs.

Cooking was really fun to me as a kid. It was the perfect match for my other hobby, eating. And making soups was just a natural evolution. It's the perfect comfort food and is pretty darn easy to prepare. It's interesting how soup manifested itself in all kinds of simple dishes back then. Onion soup mix combined with sour cream was always the perfect chip dip. Then mixing cream of mushroom soup with a can of green beans and topping it with a can of dried onion rings became popular. Let's face it: I grew up at the beginning of the convenience food age, an unfortunate trend that has muddled the diets of the western world for decades. Thank goodness my mom still showed me the methods for making things from scratch. . . well, almost completely from scratch. I have to admit when I first started making homemade pizza in high school I was using Pillsbury dough mix for the crust. I also heavily doctored up Ragu spaghetti sauce for my buddies when we held our weekly lasagna dinners in high school.

When I become a parent myself, teaching my kids to cook came naturally to me. Unlike me, however, my kids are incredibly picky eaters. It's completely my fault, because my house often resembles a restaurant and I'm the short order cook. I always thought my kids had unusual tastes for, well, kids, anyway. For instance, they have never really liked cake. But one thing is for sure, whenever I thought I had their tastes pegged, the next week they would change. In fact, teaching my kids to cook was almost a defense strategy. I knew if we were going to order pizza, that an argument was likely in order. They could never agree on toppings. As a solution, I started making pizza dough and offering a spread of various toppings. They would roll out their own dough and top it the way they wanted. They would bake it to the "doneness" they preferred. And when they

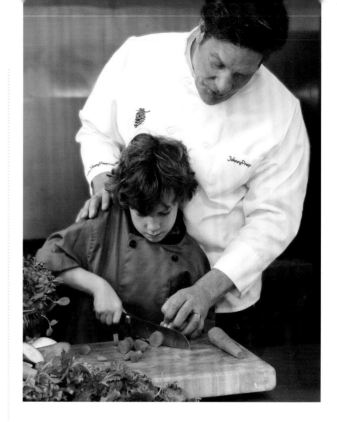

were finished, they always liked what they made. Perfect! No more arguments.

Then I had a brainstorm. My kids each had some favorite foods. Coconut shrimp, gumbo, my buffalo wings, and fresh nacho chips and salsa were amongst them. I knew there would be a point in my life where I would be going to their houses for the holidays. For all I know, I could be living with one of them in my twilight years. Rolling the dice that my in-laws would be good cooks would be a risky proposition. So I decided to teach each of my kids three tasty dishes that both they —and I—really like. Just in case I'm put out to pasture or simply stopped by for a family dinner, I know I can get something good to eat! I guess only time will tell if this strategy works.

Through the years, my experience cooking with kids has expanded dramatically. It started when I wanted to pilot a critical thinking class that I had written for ten- and eleven-year-olds. The class taught them how to use deductive logic to solve Sudoku puzzles. I had a week-long half-day camp with a small group of kids during the summer and tested out some animations as a teaching tool. The kids would come over to the house for six hours every day for a week. I knew going into it that keeping kids' attention for that amount of time every day was going to be impossible, so I needed to work in some fun activities. To that end, I decided to teach them how to cook.

One day we made pasta noodles from scratch. Another day we made homemade pizzas and the kids got to make the dough and the whole nine yards. The last day we made homemade ice cream and chocolate chip cookies. Then we constructed them into ice cream sandwiches. We discovered two things that week. One was that the kids were very capable of learning how to do Sudoku puzzles; the other was that they really liked to cook. They were actually disappointed when the classes stopped because they wanted to come back and play in the kitchen!

Many kids do enjoy cooking. It's hands on. They get to make things their way. And they get to eat it when they are done. What more could they ask for?

As a parent in the new millennium, competition for your kid's attention can be stiff. Television, computer games, and sports suck up a lot of their time, while the companies that produce these products and activities do everything they can to make them engaging for kids. Cooking represents the ideal opportunity to do something fun with your kids where you actually get to interact and spend time with them in a meaningful way.

Cooking with your kids has many benefits. It doesn't cost you anything and you're going to buy food to eat anyway. Cooking from scratch is actually a low cost alternative if you develop some shopping skills. Compare that to the cost of taking them to a movie, bowling, or golfing these days!

Preparing meals with your kids also gives you the ability to influence their healthy eating habits. Try taking your kids to a store and have them pick out a couple of vegetables. Then make a simple soup with them. I don't know anything that gets kids to eat vegetables better then soup.

It also provides your kids with a valuable life skill. It doesn't matter if you are a male or a female; the way to everyone's hearts is through their stomachs. It's easy to make friends when you're serving good food!

So do yourselves and your kids a favor—teach them how to cook. If you don't know how to cook yourself, then read my forthcoming series of books with them and go on a culinary discovery together. I'll guarantee it will add value and fun to your life!

Essential Broths & Stocks

When you think of broth, you think of soup. Right? But broth—the chef's best kept secret—isn't limited to just soup. It's often an essential ingredient in any number of your most beloved recipes, like those you will find within these pages. From the summery Beefsteak Tomato Basil Soup and creamy Shrimp Bisque to main course meals like zesty Mexican Tacos Carnitas and full-bodied Beer Braised Short Ribs, broth provides a flavor undercurrent to a variety dishes that the "home chef" can easily recreate on the dinner table, just like they do at their favorite restaurant.

Homemade, slow-cooked broth and stock is like nothing else. It's the quintessential balm for the soul and the very heart of flavor in everything from soup to entrées. Use it in your rice, pasta, and casserole or to flavor your favorite lamb, pork, chicken or seafood dish. But first, you have to start with the basics—these broth and stock recipes are the can't-do-without foundations that cooks of all skill levels can master with ease. So roll up your sleeves, grab you ladle, and simmer away!

Simple Vegetable Broth SERVES 8

This broth has such a garden fresh flavor it's worth drinking like tea!

1 large Spanish onion, cut in half
2 large carrots, peeled
1 stalk celery
1 whole turnip, sliced in 1/4 inch slices
1 whole leek, cleaned and cut in half lengthwise
3-4 sprigs parsley
1 large bay leaf
2 sprigs thyme
6 whole peppercorns
1 clove garlic
cold water

Place all ingredients in a large stock pot and cover with 1 inch cold water. Don't stir pot during the entire process. Bring to a boil over high heat. As soon as the water starts to boil, turn down the heat to a slow simmer. Simmer for 2 hours.

Carefully ladle the broth through a fine mesh strainer lined with damp cheesecloth. Broth can be seasoned for immediate use or stored in resealable plastic bags and frozen up to 3 months.

Grandma's Best Chicken Broth SERVES 8

Just like Grandma Lucy used to make!

1	whole chicken
1	large Spanish onion, cut in half
2	large carrots, peeled
1	stalk celery
3-4	sprigs parsley
	cold water

Place all ingredients in a large stock pot and cover with 1 inch cold water. Don't stir pot during the entire process. Bring to a boil over high heat. As soon as the water starts to boil, turn down the heat to a slow simmer.

Watch pot as scum starts to accumulate on surface. Using a flat ladle or large spoon, skim off scum and discard. If using right away, skim off as much fat as you can as well. Continue to skim periodically until no more scum forms and broth is clear. Simmer for 2 hours.

Carefully remove ingredients from the broth. Press on onion in pot to extract flavor as you remove. Discard onion, celery and parsley. Place chicken and carrots in a bowl to cool for later use.

At this point you can remove most of the fat by skimming and then straining through a double cheesecloth. Or if you have the time you can refrigerate until the fat forms a skin on top of the broth and you can just peel it off. This method works the best. Broth can be seasoned for immediate use or stored in resealable plastic bags and frozen for up to 3 months.

Rich Chicken Broth

The name says it all. . . but this clear, refined, and flavorful broth has an extra yet traditional kick.

1	whole chicken, seasoned and roasted
1	large Spanish onion, cut in half
2	large carrots, peeled
1	stalk celery
3-4	sprigs parsley
1	large bay leaf
2	sprigs thyme
6	whole peppercorns
1	clove garlic
	cold water

Place all ingredients in a large stock pot and cover with 1 inch cold water. Don't stir pot during the entire process. Bring to a boil over high heat. As soon as the water starts to boil, turn down the heat to a slow simmer.

Watch pot as scum starts to accumulate on surface. Using a flat ladle or large spoon, skim off scum and discard. If using right away, skim off as much fat as you can as well. Continue to skim periodically until no more scum forms and broth is clear. Simmer for 2 hours.

Carefully remove ingredients from the broth. Press on onion in pot to extract flavor as you remove. Discard everything but the broth, chicken and carrots. Place chicken and carrots in a bowl to cool for later use.

At this point you can remove most of the fat by skimming and then straining through a double cheesecloth. Or if you have the time you can refrigerate until the fat forms a skin on top of the broth and you can just peel it off. This method works the best. Broth can be seasoned for immediate use or stored in resealable plastic bags and frozen for up to 3 months.

Rich Beef Broth SERVES 8

The hearty, nourishing flavors in this beef broth recipe add depth to any dish.

2	tablespoons olive oil
2	pounds stewing beef or chuck roast (can be ground)
1	large Spanish onion, rough chopped
2	large carrots, peeled and rough chopped
1	stalk celery, rough chopped
2	tablespoons tomato paste
3-4	sprigs parsley
1	large bay leaf
2	sprigs thyme
6	whole peppercorns
2	whole allspice berries (optional)
1	clove garlic
	cold water

Heat olive oil in large stock pot over high heat. Add beef (don't crowd pan, add in batches if necessary) and brown until one side has a deep brown crust. Remove beef from pan and set aside. Add onions, celery, garlic and carrots to pan and sauté until onions are soft and translucent, stirring occasionally. Add tomato paste and cook until paste forms brown crust in bottom of pan, stirring and scraping often with a wooden spoon. Place the rest of the ingredients in a large stock pot and cover with 1 inch cold water. Don't stir pot during the entire process.

Bring to a boil over high heat. As soon as the water starts to boil, turn down the heat to a slow simmer. Watch pot as scum starts to accumulate on surface. Using a flat ladle or large spoon, skim off scum and discard. If using right away, skim off as much fat as you can as well. Continue to skim periodically until no more scum form and broth is clear. Simmer for 2 hours.

Strain broth through a strainer covered with double cheesecloth that has been moistened with water. Press on onion in pot to extract flavor as you remove. Discard everything but the broth, beef and carrots. Place beef and carrots in a bowl to cool for later use.

At this point you can remove most of the fat by skimming and then straining through a double cheesecloth. Or if you have the time you can refrigerate until the fat forms a skin on top of the broth and you can just peel it off. This method works the best. Broth can be seasoned for immediate use or stored in resealable plastic bags and frozen for up to 3 months.

Golden Consommé

Served as an appetizer or vegetable garnish, this elegant Golden Consommé is the queen of broths.

2	cups onions, chopped
1	cup carrots, chopped
1	cup celery, chopped
3	pounds lean ground beef
12	egg whites, beaten
2	tablespoons salt
10	ounces fresh or canned tomatoes, chopped
1	standard sachet
1	clove
2	allspice berries
12	cups rich chicken broth or stock, cold
1	oignons brûlée

Blend the mirepoix, ground beef, egg whites, salt, tomatoes and the sachet ingredients. Allow to macerate (soften or break up) for 1 to 2 hours if time permits. Heat the broth/stock to approximately 100 degrees. Add the clarification mixture to the broth/stock. Stir to combine thoroughly. Bring the mixture to 144 degrees, stirring frequently until the raft just begins to form, 8 to 10 minutes. Look for the proteins to start to float and form small quarter-size clumps with lighter, unclarified broth/stock between them.

Once raft forms, firmly create a small hole in part of the raft. If using the oignons brûlés, add to the broth/stock near the hole. Simmer slowly at approximately 180 degrees. The appropriate flavor and clarity is achieved in 1 to 1½ hours. Baste the raft occasionally through the opening. Always taste to make sure the consommé has developed full flavor before straining.

Strain the consommé through a damp paper filter or rinsed doubled cheesecloth. Use a ladle to push down on the raft carefully at the hole and allow the broth to flow into the ladle before pouring through the filter. Repeat until the raft hits the bottom of the pot. Carefully tilt the broth/stock into the ladle and do not break the raft. Adjust seasoning with salt as needed.

The consommé is now ready to finish, or may be rapidly cooled and refrigerated for later service. To finish the soup for service, return it to a boil. Degrease the hot consommé by skimming or blotting with paper towels, or lift the fat from the surface of the refrigerated consommé. Taste the consommé and adjust seasoning with salt. Serve in heated bowls or cups and garnish as desired.

Dashi
[Japanese Fish Stock]

Dashi, a deliciously aromatic sea broth commonly used in Japanese cooking, is super quick and easy to make.

4 large sheets kombu (8x8 inches)

4½ quarts water

4 cups katsuobushi (bonito flakes)

All these ingredients are readily available at Japanese and most oriental markets. Put kombu in a large stock pot and cover with water. Let it soak for 30 minutes. Heat the pan over medium heat until you start to see small bubbles appear but not yet to a simmer. Remove the kombu and discard. Bring to a medium boil for 8 minutes. Reduce the heat to a simmer and add bonito flakes. Simmer for 15 minutes.

Strain the liquid through several layers of cheesecloth or one layer of butter muslin that has been placed in a strainer or china cap. Let completely cool. Store in sealtight plastic bags or containers and freeze for up to 3 months. Keeps in the fridge for up to 1 week.

Seafood Stock

Flavors derived from the shells of shrimp, lobster or crab offer the home cook
a variety of seafood flavors from which to choose.

16 cups shrimp, lobster or crab shells

2 whole carrots, peeled

1 large onion, peeled and cut in half

1 large celery stock, cleaned

1 large bay leaf

8 whole black peppercorns

enough water to cover shells plus 1 inch more

Place all ingredients in a large stock pot. Cover with cold water. Bring to a boil and immediately reduce to a simmer. Simmer the stock for 2 hours. Let stock pot cool until shells are cool enough to throw in your wastebasket. Using a strainer fish out all the large shells and throw them away. Pour the remaining stock through the strainer into a large enough bowl to fit all the liquid. Let cool. Stock can be stored in seal-tight plastic bags and frozen for future use or used immediately. Can be kept well in the fridge for up to a week.

Vegetable Soups

Vegetable soup is a wonderful combination of freshness, comfort, and nutrition. If you're a gardener or farmer, or have access to any of the growing numbers of bountiful farmers markets across the country, then you're lucky enough to source your vegetables close to home. Cooking with fresh veggies makes these tasty yet healthy recipes that much more pleasurable to prepare.

If you don't grow your own, an abundance of veggies are only as far away as your local grocer. There you will find a harvest of tomatoes, beets, cabbage, broccoli, asparagus, butternut squash—you name it—the perfect ingredients for this perennial favorite. Let your imagination run wild with the various soup combinations. To get the juices flowing, think Spicy Tomato Tortelloni Soup, Roasted Golden Beet Soup, Black Bean Soup, or Swiss Onion Soup.

There are soups for all seasons—light and simple in the spring, cooling and piquant in the summer, earthy and nourishing in the fall, and robust and warming during the long cold winter. Veggies soup is, quite simply, satisfying no matter the time or place. There are endless ways to prepare this versatile, always flavorful soup staple, signaling life beyond what you find in a can.

Spicy Tomato Tortelloni Soup

You'll need to be prepared to make Bolognese sauce or buy a really good quality version. I make mine with Italian sausage.

2 cups rich chicken broth

2 cups Bolognese sauce

1 medium zucchini squash, diced

1 medium summer squash, diced

1 teaspoon chili flakes or to taste

2 cups dried cheese tortelloni (if using fresh reduce cooking time)

1 cup parmesan cheese, freshly grated

   salt and fresh ground pepper to taste

Bring broth to a boil in a soup pot. Add the pasta to the pot and boil according to the package's instructions. Two minutes before pasta is done, add pepper flakes, zucchini and summer squash to pot and bring to a boil. Simmer for 2 minutes.

Add the Bolognese sauce. Cook on simmer for five minutes. Stir in half of the parmesan cheese and stir to incorporate until cheese has melted into soup. Use rest of cheese for garnish.

Fire Roasted Tomato and Cabbage Soup

This recipe has a great body and depth of flavor for a vegetarian soup.

1   large sweet onion (like Vidalia), cut into strips

1   clove garlic clove, chopped

1   fennel bulb (white part), cut into strips

½   medium cabbage, shredded into thin strips

2   cans fire-roasted tomatoes

⅜   cup canola oil or other vegetable oil

¼   cup all-purpose flour

6   cups vegetable broth

2   tablespoons liquid smoke, hickory flavor

    salt and pepper to taste

In a large soup pan sweat together over medium heat ⅛ cup olive oil, onions, fennel and garlic until they are soft and translucent. Add cabbage to the pan and continue to sauté until cabbage is soft and tender as well. Add fire-roasted tomatoes along with the juice in the can. Continue to cook for 10 minutes until tomatoes start to break down into a sauce.

Add broth to pan and stir. Get a small frying pan very hot over high heat and add the rest of the oil. Add the flour and continuously stir (be careful, splatters from the hot oil really burn) until the flour takes on a light brown color. Remove pan from heat and place under a trickle of water in the sink and stir in enough water to make into a thick sauce. Stir this mixture back into the soup in the pot. Add liquid smoke and taste to balance salt, pepper and smoke flavor. Simmer soup for 30 minutes.

Roasted Golden Beat Soup

SERVES 6

My wife once hated beets because all she had ever had was the red canned variety. Once she tried roasted, she fell in love. The gentle sweetness of the roasted golden beats blends heavenly with the light anise flavor of the fennel. Just delicious!

6 golden beats (medium to large in size)
1 cup onion, chopped
2 cups fennel bulbs (white part), finely chopped
3 tablespoons olive oil
1 sprig rosemary
4 cups chicken or vegetable broth
salt and fresh ground pepper to taste

Preheat oven to 400 degrees. Cut leaves and roots off of golden beats and place them in a greased baking dish (foil and non-stick spray work great). Brush beets lightly with oil and place in oven. Roast for 1 hour or until they get slightly soft and skin has pulled away from flesh. Remove from oven and let cool.

Peel beets and course chop them into a dice. In a soup pan, place rest of the olive oil over medium heat. Place the onions, rosemary and fennel in the pan and season lightly with salt and pepper. Place lid on pan and sweat vegetable for 10 minutes. Remove lid and cook for 5 more minutes. Remove rosemary sprig and add golden beats to pan. Season lightly with salt and pepper. Cook for an additional 5 minutes stirring occasionally.

Add stock, bring to a boil, then reduce heat to a simmer. Simmer for 30 minutes. Using a stick blender (or food processor or regular blender), purée soup until it's velvety smooth. Give it a final taste and adjust seasoning. Garnish with thin golden beat slice and small piece of rosemary spring.

Spring Leaf Soup

4	ounces whole grain wheat pasta, enriched
5	cups rich chicken broth
2	bunches scallion greens, cut into 1 inch pieces
4	cups spinach, roughly shredded
2	cups arugula leaves (baby is preferable)
2	cups sorrel, toughly shredded
2	cups watercress leaves
¾	cup white wine
½	cup heavy cream
	salt and fresh ground pepper to taste
	extra greens for garnish

Bring stock to a boil in a soup pot. Break pasta into thirds and carefully drop into boiling water. Cook for 15 minutes or twice the manufacturer's recommendations. Add all the leaves to the pot along with the scallions and cook for another 5 minutes.

Using a stick blender, purée the soup until very smooth. This can be done in a processor or blender, but be very careful not to overfill the vessel (like ⅓). Add the wine and cream and stir to incorporate. Heat on simmer for another 3 minutes. Season to taste with salt and fresh ground pepper. Garnish with extra greens sliced very thin.

Broccoli, Sweet Pepper, and Butternut Squash Soup

SERVES 12

A beautifully complex and nutritious soup with lots of natural sweetness and a nutty undertone.

¼	cup olive oil
1	cup onion, chopped
1	cup carrots, diced
3	cups butternut squash
2	cups sweet red and yellow peppers
2	cups broccoli
2	tablespoons garlic clove, chopped
1	jalapeno chili, stemmed, seeded and finely diced
1	whole bay leaf
1	tablespoon fresh thyme, chopped
3	ounces dried pasta of your choice, cooked to al dente
12	cups chicken or vegetable broth
	salt and pepper to taste

Place oil in a big soup pot over medium heat. Add onions, carrots, butternut squash, garlic, jalapeno, bay leaf, and thyme and stir to incorporate. Season lightly with salt and fresh ground pepper. Sweat vegetables until they begin to turn slightly brown and a crust start to form on the bottom. Stir and scrape bottom to remove crust as it builds up. This should take about 20 minutes.

Add broccoli, pasta and stock and cook for another 30 minutes on a simmer. Purée soup with a stick blender until smooth. Season to taste with salt and pepper. Garnish with thin pepper slices, and very small broccoli flowerettes.

Roasted Butternut Squash Soup

1 large butternut squash
2 cups rich chicken stock
½ cup cream
 salt and pepper to taste

Preheat oven to 350 degrees. Slice squash in half length-wise. Remove seeds. Puncture outer skin several times with the point of a knife. Place squash skin side up on a half sheet pan lined with foil. Pour ½ cup water in pan. Place squash in oven and roast until outer skin is very soft and browned well. This should take at least 1 hour and possibly 1½ hours. Remove from oven and let cool.

In a large food processor with a blade, scoop out squash meat and process until very smooth. You can add ½ cup of stock to help the processing. Do this in batches if the squash is really large. Place purée in stock pot. Add stock and stir. Bring to a boil over medium high heat. Add cream and season to taste with salt and pepper.

Savory Hummus and Tomato Soup SERVES 4

The tomatoes and aromatics turn this into a wonderful Middle Eastern taste fest!

2   tablespoons olive oil

1   medium onion, chopped

2   cloves garlic, finely chopped

2   teaspoons ground cumin (best if fresh ground)

1   teaspoon cinnamon

1   teaspoon fresh ginger, grated

2   14 ounce cans chickpeas

2   tablespoons Tahini (ground sesame seeds)

1   pound ripe tomatoes, peeled and chopped

6   cups rich chicken broth or vegetable broth
    (for vegetarian)

2   tablespoons parsley, chopped fine

1   teaspoon fresh lemon juice, or to taste

Heat the oil on medium heat in a soup pan. Add the onion and garlic and cook for a few minutes until the onions are soft and translucent. Stir in the cumin, cinnamon, ginger, Tahini, chickpeas, tomatoes and the stock. Bring to a boil. Reduce to simmer and simmer for 10 minutes.

Using a stick blender (or food processor or blender, but be careful not to fill vessel more than $1/3$ with hot liquids) purée the soup until it's smooth. Add lemon juice and adjust to taste. Season with salt and fresh ground pepper to taste.

Sweet Corn Chowder

The beautiful sweetness of fresh corn really shines through, complimenting the soft crunch of the chowder.

1   whole carrot, grated
1   whole celery stick, finely chopped
1   medium onion, finely chopped
1   large red skin potato, small dice
4   ears corn, kernels cut off cobb (can use frozen)
3   tablespoons olive oil
1   whole bay leaf
2   sprigs fresh thyme, chopped
2   cans (15 ounce) creamed corn
4   tablespoons sweetened condensed milk
4   cups chicken or vegetable broth
½   cup water
2   tablespoons corn starch
    salt and freshly ground black pepper to taste

In a soup pan over medium heat, add olive oil and preheat. Add onions, carrots, celery, bay leaf, and thyme and stir. Season lightly with salt and pepper. Cook for 10 minutes, stirring occasionally until onions are soft and transparent. Add potatoes and stir. Continue to cook for 5 minutes, stirring occasionally. Season lightly with salt and pepper.

Add corn, stir, and cook for 5 more minutes. Season lightly with salt and pepper and stir occasionally, scraping the bottom to dig up the good golden stuff off the bottom (fond). Stir in both cans of creamed corn and condensed milk. Pour in broth and stir. Bring to a boil, reduce to simmer and cook for 20 minutes. Stir corn starch into water to dissolve. Add this slurry mixture to the pot, stir, and bring back to a boil. Shut off heat. Season to taste with salt and pepper.

Swiss Onion Soup

Loaded with cheese and caramelized onions, this soup is decadently delicious!
Try it with some crusty bread and a salad.

2	tablespoons olive oil
4	cups onion cut into strips
1	clove garlic clove, chopped
1	teaspoon thyme leaves
4	tablespoons butter
4	tablespoons flour
12	ounces Gruyère cheese, shredded
½	cup beer
1	teaspoon Worcestershire sauce
½	teaspoon hot sauce (Tabasco or whatever you prefer)
1	cup croutons
2	cups milk
4	cups rich chicken broth

Heat a large soup pan over medium high heat. Add oil, onions, thyme and garlic and cover for 10 minutes. Remove cover and cook for an additional 10 minutes. Add beer and continue to cook until most of beer is evaporated.

Add butter and flour and cook for 3 minutes, stirring slowly. Add milk and bring to a boil while stirring. Add cheese and stir slowly into sauce. Add chicken broth, Worcestershire, hot sauce, and season with salt and pepper to taste. Garnish with croutons.

Black Bean Soup

Remember you have to soak the beans overnight!

2 12 ounce packages black beans, dried

4 ounces Andouille (or kielbasa) sausage, diced into small pieces

1½ cups onion, diced

¾ cup green pepper, diced

2 tablespoons olive oil

1 tablespoon garlic cloves, finely chopped

½ cup jalapeno chiles, finely diced

1 tablespoon cumin seeds, ground

1 teaspoon coriander seeds, ground

½ teaspoon oregano leaves, crushed

1 teaspoon ancho chile powder

8 cups chicken broth

1 cup sour cream

salt and pepper to taste

Place dried beans in a large bowl and cover with water 2 inches above the dried beans. If beans start to bloat above water, add more water. Let soak overnight. Prior to making the soup, drain out the liquid.

In a large soup pot heat olive oil. Sauté sausage until its fat is rendered and it's nicely browned. Add all the vegetables except the beans and all the spices and herbs. Sauté over medium heat until onions are soft and translucent, about 5 minutes. Season lightly with salt and pepper. Add beans and broth and bring to a boil. Reduce heat to a simmer and cook with the cover on for 90-100 minutes or until beans are soft to the bite.

Remove 1½ cups of the beans and set aside. Using a stick blender, purée the soup mixture in the pot until it's smooth but still has good texture. Add back the whole beans. Adjust seasoning with salt and pepper. Serve with a large dollop of sour cream on each serving. Garnish with finely diced jalapenos.

Beefsteak Tomato Basil Soup

The companion ingredients of tomato and basil combined with
the cooling flavors create a unique spin on traditional garden favorites.

1   cup onions, diced

1   cup fennel bulbs (white part), finely chopped

1   teaspoon garlic clove, chopped

2   tablespoons olive oil

1   tablespoon tomato paste

5   cups beefsteak tomatoes, coarse chop

1   cup fresh basil leaves, chopped

1   tablespoon sugar

4   cups rich chicken broth or vegetable broth
    (for vegetarian)

    salt and pepper to taste

Heat olive oil in soup pot on medium high heat. Add onions and fennel and sweat for 5 minutes until onions are soft and translucent. Add garlic and cook for 2 more minutes. Add tomato paste and cook for 3 additional minutes or until tomato paste starts to brown on the bottom of the pan. Add tomatoes, basil, 1 teaspoon salt, sugar and a pinch of black pepper. Cook for 5 more minutes, stirring occasionally.

Add broth and bring to a boil. Reduce to simmer and cook for 30 minutes. Using a stick blender (or carefully using a blender or food processor), purée soup until consistent and smooth. Adjust seasoning with salt and pepper, or add even a little more sugar if tomatoes are really acidic. Serve with crouton garnish and fresh basil.

Carrot Soup SERVES 4

This is a deliciously simple soup. The key, of course, is to use a good rich chicken stock!

1 pound carrots, peeled and cut into 1-inch lengths
2 cups rich chicken stock
½ cup cream
salt and pepper to taste

Place carrots in a pot and cover with rich chicken stock. Bring to a boil and reduce to medium heat. Cook carrots until soft and fork tender.

Using a slotted spoon, take carrots and place them in a food processor with a blade attached. Reserve stock in pot. Take about ½ cup of stock and put into food processor. Process carrots until they are a very smooth puree (this might take a few minutes).

Pour carrots back into pan with reserved stock. Add cream and stir to incorporate. Bring to a low simmer and season to taste with sea salt and fresh ground pepper. You can add additional stock if you prefer your soup thinner.

Poultry, Seafood, & Other Meat

Nothing is guaranteed to satisfy more on a chilly winter's day than a big bowl of thick Shrimp Bisque or Sweet Pea and Mint Lamb Meatball Soup. With your hands around the warm dish, breathing in the heady mix of meaty aromas, anticipating the hearty taste of something new yet familiar, we cannot fault the home chef for falling in love with this traditional comfort food all over again.

On the other hand, a bowl of Lemongrass and Ginger Shrimp Soup or Fiery Cool Avocado Crab Soup represents the ideal dish to serve guests in the spring or summer when your taste buds crave something light and refreshing.

Look at the process of making soups with meat or seafood as an opportunity to free yourself of any sort of limitations you might put on yourself as a home chef. There is, in fact, no limit to what you can create because you can toss in anything you want—lamb, shrimp, pork, crab, turkey, beef, or chicken, as well as all of the "add-ons" that heighten the meaty flavors. Beans, rice, pasta, and veggies layer in texture and heartiness, while herbs, spices, and oils bring out the depth and richness of any meat or seafood-based soup. The ingredient combinations are endlessly inspiring! But, we have some ideas for you on where to start. . .

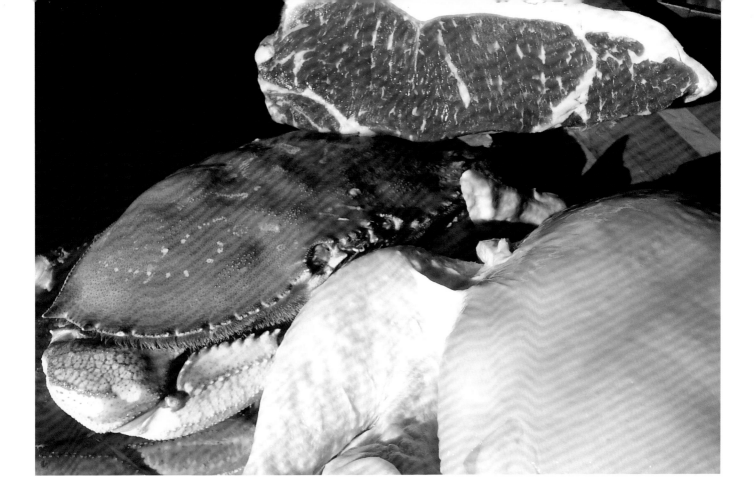

Sweet Pea and Mint Lamb Meatball Soup SERVES 4

Mixing honey Greek yogurt with mint and sweet peas is a fresh, sweet and sour delight that perfectly compliments the rich taste of lamb.

SOUP

14 ounces frozen sweet peas

2 cups rich chicken both

½ cup Greek honey yogurt

2 tablespoons seasoned rice wine vinegar

2 tablespoons fresh mint, finely chopped

    salt and ground fresh black pepper to taste

LAMB MEATBALLS

1 pound lamb, ground

1 egg, beaten

½ cup bread crumbs, preferably fresh

½ teaspoon garlic powder

½ teaspoon onion powder

¼ teaspoon black pepper, freshly ground

½ teaspoon soda water

Preheat oven to 400 degrees. Thoroughly mix all ingredients for the meatballs in a bowl. Foil and apply non-stick spray to a baking pan. Roll lamb mixture into small meatballs (1 inch or less). Place them on the baking sheet and then in the oven. Bake for 30 minutes. Remove and set aside.

Place broth, mint and vinegar in a soup pan and bring to a boil. Add peas and bring back to a boil. Boil for 2 minutes (don't overcook peas or you will lose the bright, fresh color). Remove from heat. Add the honey yogurt. Using a stick blender (or a food processor or blender, but be careful not to fill vessel over ⅓ full with hot liquids) and puree until very smooth. Season with salt and fresh ground pepper. Can be served cold or heated. Place a few meatballs in every bowl.

Shrimp Bisque

SERVES 4

This is a lush, rich-tasting soup if there ever was one,
featuring the pure flavors of seafood and all the finesse of a master chef.

1   pound shrimp shells
2   tablespoons butter
8   ounces onion, chopped
2   cloves garlic, minced
2   teaspoons paprika
2   tablespoons tomato paste
⅜   cup brandy
6   cups seafood stock
6   tablespoons butter
6   tablespoons flour
1   pound shrimp, 31-40 count, peeled, de-veined
    and chopped coarsely
1   cup heavy cream
¼   teaspoon Old Bay seasoning
1   squirt Tabasco (optional)
1   squirt Worcestershire sauce
2   ounces dry sherry

Rinse the shrimp shells thoroughly and drain them.
Sauté the shrimp shells in a medium stockpot in
2 tablespoons of butter over medium high heat for
3-4 minutes or until the shells turn bright pink.

Reduce the heat to medium and add the onions.
Sauté the onions until they are translucent, about
2 minutes. Add the garlic, paprika and tomato paste
and cook for 5 minutes until there is a sweet, cooked
tomato aroma and the shells soften slightly. Remove
the shells and set aside. Deglaze the mixture with the
brandy and reduce for 3-4 minutes until nearly dry.
Add the cooked shrimp shells back.

In a separate pot, bring the seafood stock to a boil.
In the shells pot add 6 tablespoons of the butter and
the flour and stir slowly but attentively for 5 minutes.
Add the stock and stir mixture until it comes to a
boil. Reduce to a simmer and cook for 45 minutes.
Strain mixture as thoroughly as you can, preferably
with cheesecloth. Heat the cream in the microwave
for 45 seconds. Bring bisque back to a simmer and
add cream.

In a separate sauté pan, cook the chopped shrimp
until just done and pink. Add the shrimp to the
bisque and simmer for 5 minutes. Add the rest of
the seasonings and adjust to taste with salt and fresh
ground pepper. Just prior to serving add the sherry
and simmer for 1 minute.

Fiery Cool Avocado Crab Soup SERVES 6

This soup offers a wonderful balance of silky smooth body, light citrus flavor, chunks of beautiful seafood, and a touch of garden fresh zing!

SOUP

- 2 large avocados (use 3 or 4 if they are small)
- ½ pound lump crab meat
- 1 jalapeno chili, stemmed, seeded and finely diced
- 1 small garlic clove, chopped
- 6 cups chicken broth
- 1 lime juice, freshly squeezed
- 2 tablespoons sour cream
  salt and freshly ground black pepper to taste

PICO DE GALLO

- 2 ripe Roma tomatoes, diced into ¼ inch cubes
- ¼ cup red onion, finely diced
- 1 jalapeno chilies, stemmed, seeded and finely diced
- 2 tablespoons cilantro, finely chopped
- ½ lime juice, freshly squeezed

In a small bowl toss the salsa ingredients together. Season with salt and pepper to taste and set aside. Cut each avocado in half lengthwise and remove the seed. Scoop the flesh out with a large spoon and place in a food processor with a blade. Add the chilies, garlic, lime juice, sour cream and stock and then process until smooth. Season to taste with salt and pepper.

Ladle one cup of soup in a bowl and then top with a ¼ cup of lump crab. Top the crab with Pico de Gallo and sprinkle some extra decoratively on the soup.

Chicken Vegetable Soup SERVES 8

A home cook's staple, this perennial favorite is full of garden fresh vegetables and invigorating seasonings.

8	cups chicken stock
2	cups broccoli florets, cut into small pieces
2	cups green beans. sliced into 1 inch pieces
2	carrots, reserved from making stock, cut into rounds
¼	cup olive oil
8	ounces button mushrooms, sliced
2	cloves garlic, chopped fine
1	small summer squash, cut into thin rounds
1	small zucchini squash, cut into thin rounds
1	tablespoon Italian seasoning (or fresh rosemary and thyme)
	salt and pepper

Place stock in a large stock pot and bring to a boil. While stock is heating, bring a large sauté pan up to a medium high heat. Place olive oil along with mushrooms and garlic. Cook until mushrooms are very tender and starting to brown, stirring occasionally. Season lightly with salt and pepper. Add summer squash, zucchini and Italian seasoning. Season again lightly with salt and pepper. Continue cooking until squash is soft and tender. Remove pan from heat and set aside.

When stock comes to a boil, add green beans and cook for 3 minutes, then add broccoli and cook for another 5 minutes. Reduce heat to a simmer and add carrots and cooked vegetables that were sautéed back into stock pot and cook for another 5 minutes. Adjust salt and pepper to taste. At this point you can add back the diced chicken from the stock and cooked noodles of your choice.

Creamy Chicken and Rice Soup SERVES 8

1	stick butter
1	cup onion, finely chopped
1	clove garlic, minced
½	cup carrots, peeled and diced fine
½	cup celery, diced fine
½	cup flour
8	cups rich chicken broth
1	squirt Worcestershire sauce
1	squirt Tabasco (optional)
1½	cup wild rice cooked according to package directions
8	ounces cooked chicken, diced
2	cups heavy cream
	salt and pepper

Melt butter in a large soup pot over medium heat. Add onions, carrots, celery and garlic and sauté until onions are translucent and soft, about 8 minutes. Stir in flour and continue to cook while stirring for 3 minutes. Add rich chicken broth and bring to a boil, stirring occasionally. Reduce the heat to a simmer. Stir in cream (do not bring to a high boil after this). Season with Worcestershire and Tabasco. Season to taste with salt and pepper. Stir in chicken and rice. Heat on simmer for 3 minutes and serve.

Mushroom and Wild Rice Soup with Sage Meatballs

SERVES 8

This savory mushroom and vegetable broth soup uses organic whole grains and lean turkey to keep things healthy.

TURKEY MEATBALLS

1½	pounds ground turkey
1	teaspoon salt
½	teaspoon garlic power
½	teaspoon onion powder
¼	teaspoon black pepper, freshly ground
2	teaspoons fresh sage, finely chopped
¼	cup bread crumbs, preferable fresh
1	egg, beaten
¼	cup soda water

SOUP

1	ounce dried mushrooms, preferably shiitake
1	package beech mushrooms, (or 4 ounces of mushrooms of your choice)
2	tablespoons olive oil
1	small zucchini squash, diced
1	red pepper, roasted, peeled and diced
½	cup scallions cut thinly on an angle
1	cup black or wild rice
1	clove garlic, chopped
	salt and pepper to taste

Preheat oven to 400 degrees. Take dried mushrooms and place them in a bowl with boiling water. Place a plate on them to keep them submerged and soak for a least 30 minutes or longer. Drain off the stock without residue and set aside. Thinly slice mushrooms and set aside.

Take all meatball ingredients and thoroughly mix them together in a bowl. Using a 1 ounce scoop, make small meatballs no larger than 1 inch in diameter. Place them on a non-stick backing surface (or foil with non-stick spray) and put them in the oven for 18 minutes. Remove and set aside.

While meatballs are baking and mushrooms are soaking, bring 1¾ water to a boil with 1 cup of black or wild rice. Once it comes to a boil lower the heat to a simmer and cover. Cook for 35-40 minutes. Turn off heat, fluff with a fork, and let steam for 5 more minutes.

Heat a soup pan on medium heat for 2 minutes. Add oil, scallions, garlic, and both mushrooms and sauté for 5 minutes. Add a light sprinkling of salt and fresh ground pepper. Add zucchini and red peppers and continue to cook for another 3 minutes, stirring occasionally (don't stir too hard or you will break the beech mushrooms). Add the broth and meatballs and simmer for 20 minutes. Add the rice and cook for an additional 10 minutes. Season to taste with salt and fresh ground pepper. Place 4 to 5 meatballs in every bowl and spoon broth over them until just covered.

Lemongrass and Ginger Shrimp Soup

This aromatic soup is light and refreshing and brings a burst of subtle flavor to your mouth!

2   tablespoons canola oil (or other low saturated fat oil)

2   scallions, finely chopped

2   teaspoons fresh ginger, grated

1   jalapeno chili, stemmed, seeded and finely diced

1   tablespoon Thai green curry paste

5   cups chicken or vegetable broth

2   ounces noodles (angel hair or thin spaghetti works well)

2   teaspoons brown sugar

½   lime, juiced

1   pound raw shrimp, whatever size you prefer (I use 26-30/lbs)

6   ounces bean sprouts

1   bunch scallions cut thinly on an angle

1   cup cilantro, loosely packed

1   4 inch stalk lemongrass, smashed once with a cooking mallet

    salt and pepper to taste

Heat the oil on medium in a soup pot. Add the finely minced scallions, ginger, chili and curry paste and sauté for 2 minutes or until onions are getting soft. Add the lemongrass and stir in the stock. Bring to a boil, cover, and simmer for 10 minutes. While simmering, cook the noodles in a separate pan of boiling salted water until they are fully cooked. Drain and set aside.

Stir in the sugar and lime juice (save a couple of lime slices for garnish) into the broth. Add the shrimp and simmer for another 5 minutes. Add the noodles and cook for another 2 minutes. Remove the lemongrass stalk. Add the bean sprouts (save a few for garnish) and scallions and stir in ¾ of the cilantro (save the rest for garnish). Simmer for another minute or so. Season to taste with salt and pepper. Ladle into soup bowls, garnish, and serve.

Shrimp Chowder

12 ounces raw bacon, chopped

2 large yellow onions, chopped

3 tablespoons pickled jalapeño peppers

6 tablespoons butter or olive oil

½ cup whole wheat flour

½ teaspoon turmeric

1 tablespoon cumin

10 cups chicken stock

3 cups Yukon Gold potatoes, diced (skins may be left on)

10 ears fresh corn, cut off cob or 4 cups prepared

2 pounds shrimp, shelled and chopped (3 cups)

1 red pepper, diced

1 pint heavy cream (2 cups)

pinch cayenne pepper

½ teaspoon fresh ground black pepper

1-2 teaspoons sea salt

Cook chopped bacon on medium heat in large heavy bottom pot until crisp. Remove bacon and add onions and butter. Cook until onions are translucent. Stir in flour, jalapeño and spices. Add stock and potatoes. Simmer until potatoes are tender. Add corn, shrimp and cream. Season with cayenne pepper, salt and pepper and garnish with chopped bacon.

Seafood and Sausage Gumbo SERVES 6

This classic Cajun dish is designed for sharing (although no one could blame you if you helped yourself to a heaping bowl of southern-stewed goodness).

SEASONING MIX

½	teaspoon white pepper
½	teaspoon black pepper
½	teaspoon cayenne pepper
½	teaspoon thyme, crushed
¼	teaspoon oregano
2	bay leaves
2	tablespoons salt

GUMBO

¾	cup vegetable oil
¾	cup all-purpose flour
2	cups onion, chopped
1	stalk celery, chopped
1	large green bell pepper, chopped
1	tablespoon garlic clove, chopped
1	pound Andouille (or kielbasa) sausage, sliced into rounds
2	pounds shrimp, 21-25 count, peeled and de-veined
1	pound sea scallops, halved with tough part of muscle removed
1	pint fresh shucked oysters (optional)
1	pound lump crab meat
1	cup okra, diced into rounds
6	cups seafood stock (clam broth can be substituted)
2	cups white rice, cooked

Mix seasoning mixture in a small bowl and set aside.

Preheat a large frying pan over high heat for 5 minutes (do not use a non-stick pan). Add oil and preheat for 1 minute or until oil starts to lightly smoke. Carefully whisk in flour using a large whisk. Whisk constantly all over pan in a medium slow motion to prevent flour from burning in spots. Keep whisking until flour is a deep reddish brown. Be patient. A dark roux really gives this dish a tremendous depth of flavor. You will notice the roux beginning to get crumbly in texture, then it will smooth out again. Once it becomes smooth again you are close to being done.

Add half of onions, celery and green peppers to roux and stir for one minute. Add the other half along with garlic. Turn heat down to medium high and continue to stir for 3 minutes. Add spice mixture and stir to incorporate. Cook for 1 additional minute. Remove from heat and set aside.

Bring seafood stock to a boil in large pot. Stir in roux mixture until incorporated and bring back to a boil over high heat. Add sausage and cook for 10 minutes. Add shrimp and cook for 3 minutes. Add scallops and cook for 5 minutes. Add oysters, crab and okra and cook for another 5 minutes. Gumbo is traditionally served over cooked white rice.

Smokey Truffled Asparagus Soup SERVES 6

This is a luxurious soup that can stand well with the finest of meals. The fresh spring asparagus is hinted with smoke, truffles and a slight balance of herb d' Provence.

2   tablespoons olive oil

1   small smoked turkey wing or leg

½   cup carrots, diced

1   cup onions, diced

½   cup celery, diced

1   bay leaf

1   sprig fresh thyme

2   ounces dried pasta of your choice

2   pounds asparagus spears, skin peeled

½   teaspoon white truffle oil

¼   teaspoon herb d' Provence

4   cups chicken or vegetable broth

     salt and pepper to taste

Heat a soup pot to medium heat and add the oil. Add the carrots, onions, celery, and smoked meat and sweat vegetables until soft and translucent, about 10 minutes. Season lightly with salt and pepper. Add the asparagus, bay leaf, thyme, truffle oil and pasta and sauté for 10 more minutes, stirring occasionally. Add the broth and bring to a boil. Reduce heat immediately to a simmer and cover.

After 15 minutes of simmering remove the smoked meat and reserve for other purposes. Cook for another 15 minutes covered. Remove bay leaf and use a stick blender to purée the soup until it's smooth and silky. Do a final taste and season with salt and pepper. Garnish with asparagus spears that have been blanched.

Chicken Cobbler SERVES 4-6

⅓ cup butter

⅓ cup whole grain flour

⅓ cup diced onion

½ teaspoon salt

¼ teaspoon fresh ground pepper

1¾ cups chicken stock

⅔ cup milk

2½-3 cups cooked chicken, torn into bite-size pieces

¾ cup of small diced carrots

¾ cup frozen peas

2 tablespoons fresh chopped parsley

Melt butter over medium and stir in flour, onion, salt and pepper. Cook, stirring constantly until bubbly. Add stock and milk. Bring to a boil, stirring constantly. Add chicken, vegetables and parsley. Pour into greased 10 inch round casserole dish.

CARROT COBBLER TOPPING

1½ cups all-purpose flour

½ cup coarsely shredded carrot

¼ cup finely shredded zucchini

½ tablespoon baking powder

¼ teaspoon salt

¼ teaspoon fresh ground pepper

⅔ cup milk

1 tablespoon melted butter

In a medium bowl, mix flour, baking powder, salt and pepper with a whisk. Then add the carrot and zucchini and mix with a spoon. Add milk and butter and stir until moist. Don't overwork the batter; it's almost like a biscuit dough. Drop by spoonful on top of chicken and vegetables. Bake at 350 degrees for 25 minutes.

Healthy & Wholesome

We all need our vitamins and minerals. And one of the most taste bud-tantalizing ways to super-charge our health is by whipping up a broth-based dish using some of the freshest, most nutritious ingredients around.

Modern living often tempts us as consumers to overly rely on convenient, fast food as the basis of our fare, when the alternative—preparing our own equally scrumptious lunch or dinner—seems like a chore. It's not. When you take a little time to prepare your own meals, you not only nourish your body, but also your knowledge of where your food comes from. You get to know intimately what exactly goes into your body as you select each and every ingredient that makes up your dish.

The African Quinoa Soup with Turkey and Vegetables is the perfect example of a recipe that packs in the nutrients without sacrificing flavor. The ginger, scallions and jalapeño chili provide a healthy kick, while the lemongrass and lime juice add a zesty contrast to the broth. Finish off with shrimp, noodles, and seasonings, and spoon in an aromatic mouthful of pure, wholesome goodness.

African Quinoa Soup
with Turkey and Vegetables

The rich and earthy ingredients in this wholesome, nutrient-dense soup
will have you going back for seconds—and thirds.

3	cups of cooked turkey or chicken torn into bite-size pieces
3–4	tablespoons butter or olive oil
1	large onion, chopped
4	cloves minced garlic
2	small jalapenos minced or 4 tablespoons of canned green chilies
2	red bell peppers, diced
3	celery stalks, diced
1	large or 2 small zucchinis, medium diced
1	sweet potato, medium diced
2	teaspoons ground cumin
2	teaspoons dried oregano or 4 teaspoons fresh
10	cups of chicken broth
¾	cup quinoa, rinsed
¾	cup of chunky organic peanut butter
1	teaspoon sea salt
½	teaspoon fresh cracked pepper

In a heavy bottom soup pot, melt butter or oil. Add onion, garlic, jalapeno, red pepper, celery, zucchini, sweet potato, cumin and oregano. Sauté 10-15 minutes until vegetables are fragrant and onions are translucent. Add stock, quinoa, salt, pepper and cayenne pepper. Bring to boil and reduce heat to a simmer. Simmer until quinoa is cooked and vegetables are tender. Add peanut butter and turkey. Blend in completely. Simmer another 10 minutes. Taste and adjust seasonings.

Apple Squash Soup with Turkey Sausage SERVES 6

Soon to become a dinner table mainstay, the combination of apple, squash, turkey, sausage and vibrant seasonings represent all of the best flavors of fall.

1   butternut squash, halved and seeded (1½ pounds)

½   cup diced squash, roasted and reserved for garnish on top of soup

1   acorn squash, halved and seeded

½   spaghetti squash, seeded

3   tablespoons butter

1   large sweet white onion, chopped

3   cloves garlic, minced

1   tablespoon fresh ginger root, minced

2   teaspoons curry powder

3   Granny Smith apples, peeled, cored and diced medium

2   cups apple cider

4   cups chicken broth

2   teaspoons sea salt

½   teaspoon fresh ground pepper (optional)

½   teaspoon ground cinnamon

    pinch cayenne pepper to taste (optional)

GARNISH

4   links cooked apple turkey sausage, cut on bias in half inch slices

1   cup sour cream or whole milk yogurt

Preheat oven to 400 degrees. Place squash cut side down on baking sheets and roast for 45 minutes or until flesh is soft. Scoop flesh into a large bowl.

Melt butter or olive oil in a 5 quart saucepan over medium heat. Add onion and cook until translucent. Add garlic, ginger and curry powder. Cook 1 minute. Add apples, cinnamon and apple cider. Simmer for 10 minutes or until apples are soft. Add apples to squash and add broth.

In small batches puree the squash mixture with emersion in pot or small batches in food processor or blender until smooth. Return to heat and season to taste with salt, pepper and cayenne pepper. Serve soup into desired bowls and top with 3 slices of bias cut turkey sausage, small dollop of yogurt and a teaspoon of roasted diced squash.

Autumn Chicken Stew

This recipe may seem like the perfect dish for the harvest—and it is—but it should also be featured prominently on your dinner table throughout the year, thanks to its nourishing yet stimulating vegetable and seasoning variety.

	cooked chicken meat from 1 whole roasted chicken
1	medium onion, diced
2	stalks celery, diced
1½	cups apple cider
2	tablespoons butter or olive oil
6	cups chicken or veggie stock
2	small turnips, peeled and chopped
1	large sweet potato, peeled and chopped
3	large carrots, peeled and diced medium
3	parsnips (washed well, no need to peel), diced medium
1	cup rutabaga or 1 small whole, peeled and chopped
2	whole cloves, minced
½	teaspoon cinnamon
½	teaspoon ginger
3-4	tablespoons arrowroot dissolved in a couple ounces of cold water (slurry)

In a heavy bottom stockpot, heat butter or oil and sauté onions and garlic until golden brown. Add cloves, cinnamon and ginger and stir to incorporate. Deglaze pan with ¾ cup apple cider. Add chicken broth and remaining vegetables. Reduce heat to medium low and simmer for an hour, stirring occasionally. Add cooked chicken and season with salt and pepper and continue to simmer for another 10-15 minutes until veggies are cooked. Stir in a couple of tablespoons of arrowroot slurry at a time until the thickness you desire is achieved. (Remember you won't be able to tell the effect of the slurry until it comes to a boil.)

Mediterranean Lentil Soup

2 tablespoons olive oil

1 small onion, diced

3 stalks celery

2 carrots

2 cups organic lentils (soaked for 6 hours, optional)

1 bunch Swiss chard

1 teaspoon toasted cumin seeds or
   2 teaspoons ground cumin

½ teaspoon allspice

4 plum tomatoes, diced

3 tablespoons tomato paste

8 cups chicken broth

   juice of 2 fresh organic lemons and rind of one

   sea salt and fresh cracked pepper

4 links cooked lamb sausage (optional) or
   add 1 pound raw in the first stage with onions,
   celery and carrots

Sauté onions, celery, carrot and garlic in olive oil. Add soaked lentils, chicken broth, spices, lemon juice and rind, tomato paste and diced tomatoes. Simmer for 20 minutes. Add chopped Swiss chard and cook another 5 minutes. Adjust seasonings. Ladle soup into desired bowls, garnished with lamb sausage.

Chicken Minestrone SERVES 8

"Rich" and "thick" are common descriptives that define minestrone, and for good reason. This traditional Italian dish centers on the flavors of hearty chicken broth, as well as all of the abundance of the season's best garden produce.

3	tablespoons butter or oil
1	medium onion, chopped (1 cup)
2	stalks celery
1	small zucchini, chopped (1 cup)
½	cup carrots, chopped
2-4	cloves garlic, minced
6	cups chicken broth
1	can northern white beans
1	cup cooked chicken, torn or diced
1	14 ounce can diced tomatoes or 2 cups fresh diced tomatoes
2	tablespoons fresh parsley, chopped
1	tablespoon fresh oregano, chopped or ½ teaspoon of dried
1½	teaspoon sea salt
½	teaspoon fresh ground pepper
1	teaspoon fresh basil, chopped or ½ teaspoon dried
½	teaspoon fresh thyme or ¼ teaspoon dried thyme
3	cups fresh baby spinach
½	cup green beans, cut into 1 inch pieces
1	cup cooked brown rice or whole grain shell pasta fresh grated parmesan to garnish

Heat butter or oil in a heavy bottom soup pot over medium heat. Add vegetables and garlic and sauté for 5 minutes or until onion is translucent. Add broth, tomatoes, beans, green beans, chicken and spices. Bring to boil, then reduce heat and simmer 20 minutes. Add spinach and rice or pasta and simmer for 2 minutes. Garnish with shredded Parmesan cheese (optional). If using rice, add before vegetables. If using pasta, add after vegetables.

Thai Noodle Soup with Turkey Meatballs SERVES 8

The tender, herbal flavors of the turkey meatballs set off perfectly the sweet yet zesty flavors of the Thai noodle soup.

3	cups chicken stock
1	cup fresh shitake mushrooms, sliced
1	lemongrass stalk or 3 tablespoons prepared lemongrass
4	Kaffir lime leaves (fresh or frozen)
½	cup julienne carrot strips
½–¾	teaspoon dried crushed chili peppers or 2-3 whole
1	cup unflavored coconut milk
2	tablespoons lime juice, fresh squeezed
3	tablespoons fish sauce
½	teaspoon lime zest
½	teaspoon fresh ginger root, peeled and finely grated
1½	teaspoons sea salt
1	teaspoon fresh ground pepper
1–2	tablespoons brown sugar

TURKEY MEATBALLS

1	pound ground turkey
3	teaspoons minced ginger
2	teaspoons Thai green curry paste
1	teaspoon fish sauce
1	egg
¼	cup cilantro
¾	teaspoon sea salt

GARNISH

5 tablespoons scallions, bias cut

5-6 cilantro leaves

5-6 basil leaves

a few turkey meatballs

wheat or rice noodles, optional

small twist of prepared rice noodles

PROCEDURE (SOUP):

Bring chicken stock, chili peppers and Kaffir to a medium simmer for 15 minutes. Reduce heat to low simmer and add ginger, fish sauce, coconut milk, carrots, mushrooms and scallions. Simmer for an additional few minutes. Add lime juice. Garnish each bowl/portion with turkey meatballs, fresh basil leaves, green onions and coriander leaves.

PROCEDURE (TURKEY MEATBALLS):

Mix all ingredients. Roll 1 ounce meatballs and place in baking dish. Add a cup of broth from soup, cover with foil and bake at 350° for 15 minutes or until meatballs are cooked through. Return broth to soup.

Roasted Corn Tortilla Soup SERVES 6

When you have a craving for something rustic yet hearty, nothing satiates quite like a fragrant bowl full of the sunny, robust flavors of bean, corn, chicken, and tomato.

1	ear corn, shucked
1	Pablano chili
2	tablespoons olive oil
1½	pounds boneless, skinless chicken breast halves, cubed into ½ inches
2	teaspoons cumin seeds, ground
1	teaspoon coriander seeds, ground
½	teaspoon oregano leaves, crushed
2	teaspoons salt
1	medium onion, chopped
1	tablespoon garlic cloves, finely chopped
1	tablespoon tomato paste
7	cups rich chicken broth
2	tablespoons corn flour or Maseca
½	cup cilantro, finely chopped
1	lime juice, freshly squeezed
6	corn tortillas, cut into ¼-inch strips
1	avocado, preferably Hass, cut into ½-inch dice
½	cup sour cream
1	teaspoon chipotle peppers, in Adobe sauce, chopped
⅛	teaspoon salt

Over either a gas burner or grill, brown the outside of the corn until nicely browned all over. Let cool, then remove kernels from cob and set aside. Place Pablano pepper over the same flames and rotate until black all over. Place pepper in a paper bag or sealed container for 5 minutes. Using a sharp knife, scrape the char off the pepper to peel the skin. Remove stem and seeds and dice. Set aside.

Mix together sour cream, chipotle pepper, and ⅛ teaspoon salt and set aside.

In a soup pot, heat the oil over medium high heat. Mix together the seasoning and spices and sprinkle all over chicken. In batches, brown the chicken until almost cooked thru. Add all the chicken back to the pan with the onions and garlic and continue to cook for 5 minutes while stirring occasionally. Add the tomato paste and cook until it browns the bottom of the pan. Scrape the brown with a wooden spoon while stirring. Add the stock, Pablano pepper, and most of the corn (reserve some for garnish). Bring to a boil, reduce to simmer for 20 minutes.

Stir flour into the last cup of broth. Pour slurry into soup and stir to incorporate. Bring back to a boil, then reduce heat and simmer for 10 more minutes. Stir in lime juice and cilantro. Season to taste with salt and pepper. Garnish with avocado, tortilla strips, cilantro and chipotle cream.

Miso Soup

1   12 ounces firm silken tofu block
2   quarts dashi
8   tablespoons dark or red miso paste
4   tablespoons light or white miso paste
4   scallions, cut thinly on an angle
1   tablespoon salt

Drain tofu by placing it between paper towels and two plates. Place a large can on top of the top plate. Let drain for half an hour. Cut tofu into 3/8 inch pieces and set aside.

Place dashi in a large stock pot. Slowly bring to a simmer. When liquid is warm to the touch, move 2 cups of the dashi into a separate bowl. Whisk the miso paste into the 2 cups until smooth and set aside. Continue to bring the dashi to a slow simmer. Do not ever bring the liquid to a full boil. If you add the miso mixture to dashi when it's too hot it will degrade the flavor of the miso significantly. Once dashi is simmering slowly add in the miso mixture and whisk it in until it is incorporated. Add the tofu, salt and the scallions and simmer for another minute. Serve immediately.

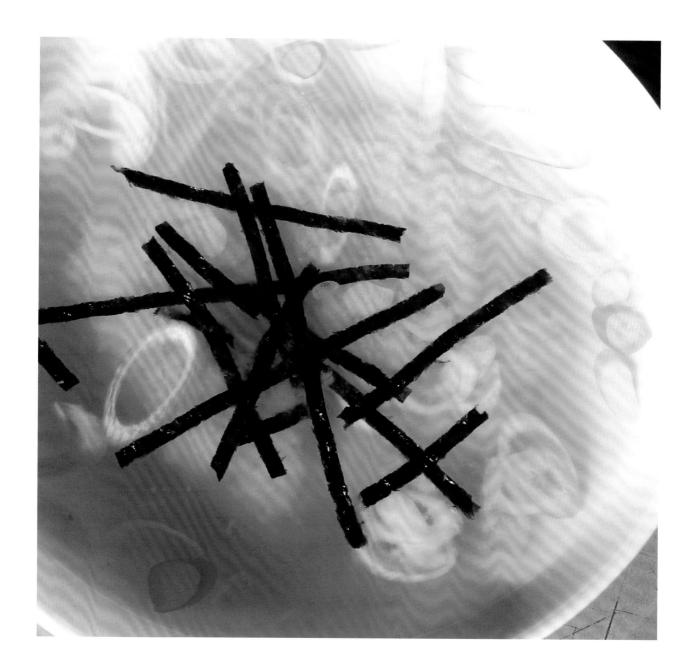

Turkey Stuffed Cabbage SERVES 8-10

2 pounds ground turkey

½ cup diced onions

1 medium head of green cabbage

1 Spanish onion, julienned

1 can diced tomatoes (14 ounces)

1 cup chicken stock

4 cloves garlic, minced

3 ounces Braggs organic apple cider vinegar

1 bay leaf

1½ teaspoons sea salt

1 teaspoon fresh ground black pepper

PROCEDURE (GROUND TURKEY):

Cook onion in oil for 1 minute, add ground turkey, and season with sea salt and pepper. Cook over medium heat, stirring often until cooked. Mix cooked turkey with cooked country style brown rice and ¾ cup of tomato basil sauce (see recipes on next page).

PROCEDURE (CABBAGE):

Preheat oven to 375 degrees. With a large knife cut cabbage in half and take core out. Place cut side down and slice the half cabbage into 6-8 large thick wedges. Repeat with other side. In overlapping layers (or "shingle"), place cabbage into large baking dish or pan. Add onions, cider vinegar, chicken stock, bay leaf and tomatoes. Season liberally with sea salt and pepper. Cover with foil and bake at 375 degrees for about 45 minutes. Prepare rice mixture and tomato basil sauce recipe.

Cabbage should be translucent and medium soft to touch. Reduce oven to 350 degrees. Drain braising liquid from cabbage into a pot and reduce liquid by half. Stir in prepared tomato sauce. Ladle ½ cup of tomato sauce onto bottom of deep 9 x 13 baking dish. Overlap and layer about half of the prepared cabbage in pan. Spread rice turkey mixture evenly over base layer of cabbage. Top turkey rice mixture with ¾ cup of tomato. Cover rice mixture with a thick layer of cabbage and top with an additional ¾ cup prepared tomato sauce. Cover with foil and bake 30 minutes at 350 degrees until cabbage is soft. This is a great dish to prep days ahead and it freezes well.

TOMATO BASIL SAUCE

- 3 cloves fresh garlic, minced
- ½ Spanish onion, diced
- ¼ cup virgin olive oil
- 2 cups tomato sauce or puree
- 2 cups tomatoes, diced (or 1 can organic tomatoes, diced)
- 4 tablespoons fresh chopped basil
- 2 teaspoons sea salt
- 1 teaspoon fresh ground black pepper

Sauté onion and garlic in olive oil. Add tomato product, sea salt and pepper. Simmer for 20 minutes on low heat. Pull from heat and add chopped basil. Adjust seasonings.

COUNTRY STYLE BROWN RICE

- 1 cup country style brown rice medley (Lundeberg would be a great choice)
- 2 cups chicken stock
- 1½ teaspoons sea salt
- ½ teaspoon pepper

Preheat oven to 375 degrees. Season stock with sea salt and pepper. Mix rice, stock and seasoning. Bake covered in oven for 45 minutes or on stove top on low heat in covered pot for 35-45 minutes or until rice is tender.

Main Courses & Entrées

In a classical kitchen, cooking broths and stocks is one of the first culinary techniques you learn. Just like in the best restaurants, this age-old fundamental technique is easy to learn but will give your friends and family the impression that you've spent all day laboring away in the kitchen.

Whether you hunger for dishes that are simple yet traditional like Whole Wheat Pasta with Fresh Tomato Meat Sauce, or a little something more mouth-wateringly adventurous, like Beer Braised Short Ribs or Chicken and Basil Dumplings, broth and stock not only bring out the distinct aromatics of your ingredients but also the tender, substantive flavors of meats and pastas. These are dishes you can serve to your family, a large gathering of friends, or even an intimate party of two.

Broth and stock can no longer be relegated to the back burner, so to speak. The art and science of making these delicious liquid flavorizers have been refined through the centuries, yet still, they retain the old-world goodness that make them timeless ingredients for today's everyday lunch or dinner fare.

Chicken and Basil Dumplings

Like two peas in a pod, basil and chicken were meant to be together.
This has become an absolute family favorite!

¼ cup butter

2 whole chickens, cut in parts

½ cup onion, chopped

¼ cup celery, chopped

1 garlic clove, chopped

¼ cup flour

4 cups rich chicken broth

1 teaspoon sugar

2 teaspoons salt

¼ teaspoon black pepper

1 teaspoon basil, dried

2 whole bay leaves

DUMPLINGS

2 cups all-purpose biscuit mix (like Bisquick)

1 teaspoon basil, dried

⅔ cup milk

Heat butter in a large skillet. Add chicken pieces and brown on all sides. Remove chicken from skillet. Add onion, celery and garlic to skillet. Cook until vegetables are tender. Sprinkle with flour and mix well. Add chicken broth, sugar, salt, pepper, basil, and bay leaves. Bring to a boil, stirring constantly. Return chicken to the skillet and spoon sauce over it. Cover pan with lid. Cook in a 350 degree oven for 40 minutes.

In a bowl, combine biscuit mix, basil and milk and stir with fork until fully incorporated. Remove pan chicken from oven and turn up temperature to 425 degrees. Stir peas into mixture. Using a tablespoon, drop dumplings on to the top of the chicken mixture so that they sit in the sauce. Return to oven and cook uncovered for 10 minutes. Place cover on and cook for an additional 10 minutes.

Bacon and Feta Stuffed Pork Chops

Your mouth is watering already, right? Feta, bacon, and pork chops. Enough said.

4   10-12 ounces double cut pork chops
1   tablespoon olive oil
1   tablespoon salt
½   teaspoon ground black pepper
½   teaspoon garlic powder
½   teaspoon paprika
4   ounces button mushrooms, sliced thin
¼   cup cooked bacon, rough chopped
1   teaspoon thyme
4   tablespoons butter
¾   cup onion, finely chopped
1   tablespoon garlic clove, chopped
1   cup bread, cubed
½   cup chicken stock or canned chicken broth
½   cup feta cheese, crumbled
    salt and pepper to taste

Melt butter over medium heat in sauté pan. Add onions and garlic and sauté until onions are translucent. Add mushrooms, thyme and bacon and continue cooking until mushrooms are very soft, stirring occasionally. Add bread and stir aggressively. Cook for 3 minutes. Add stock and stir aggressively again. Stir in feta cheese and remove from heat. Season with salt and pepper to taste. Set aside.

Brush chops with olive oil and season with salt, pepper, garlic powder and paprika. Preheat grill pan over medium high heat and lightly coat with olive oil. Place chops in pan in batches and grill until you have nice grill marks on both sides of chops.

Preheat oven to 350 degrees. Take a sharp boning knife and cut a pocket in each chop. Overfill each chop with stuffing and place on a foil lined and oiled baking sheet. Bake for 25 minutes or until your temperature of choice.

Mushroom Parmesan Risotto

SERVES 4

This has the rich mushroom flavor you find in fine Italian restaurants.

4 ounces dried mushrooms, preferably Porcinis

6 cups rich chicken broth

8 ounces button mushrooms, sliced
(wild mushrooms are a great sub)

4 tablespoons olive oil

2 cups Arborio rice

½ cup Parmesano Reggiano cheese, grated
salt and fresh ground pepper to taste

Place two cups of stock in a small pot and bring to a boil. Place dried mushrooms in a bowl and pour hot stock over them. Place a weight such as a plate on top of them to keep them submerged. Let them steep for 30 minutes. Remove steeping mushrooms and place in a food processor and puree. Set aside.

Reserve mushroom-infused broth by pouring it off into a large measuring cup, making sure not to pour in the sediment. Set aside.

Heat 2 tablespoons of olive oil in a sauté pan over medium high heat and add the fresh mushrooms and the garlic. Season lightly with salt and pepper. Reduce the heat to medium and stir occasionally. Cook until mushrooms are thoroughly cooked and browned with all the water having been absorbed. Add the pureed mushrooms, stir, and cook for 3 more minutes.

Heat chicken and mushroom stocks together in a small pan on simmer. In a large sauté pan heat 2 tablespoons olive oil on medium high heat until hot. Add rice and stir for 1 minute until rice turns more opaque. Add 1 cup broth and slowly stir until most of the moisture has been evaporated. (Be patient!) Add another cup and keep stirring. You will continue this procedure for 15 minutes. If you run out of liquid you can start using hot water.

After 15 minutes, add the mushroom mixture. Continue to cook, adding and evaporating liquid for 7 more minutes. Stir in butter and cream. Stir in parmesan cheese. Season with salt and pepper to taste. Serve immediately. Garnish with extra cheese.

Weekday Paella

This is a great Paella with tons of flavor, but it doesn't mean you have to shop for a safari of exotic ingredients!

10 cups chicken stock or canned chicken broth

¼ cup olive oil

1 whole chicken, cut into 10 pieces

2 cups onion, finely chopped

3 tablespoons garlic clove, finely chopped

1 cup red bell pepper, seeded and chopped

2 tablespoons Italian seasoning

1 pound Kielbasa or smoked sausage, cut into 1 inch pieces

1 cup green peas, frozen

1 pound shrimp, 21–25 count, peeled and de-veined

2 cups white rice uncooked

salt and freshly ground black pepper

Season chicken thoroughly with salt and pepper. Preheat a large broad paella pan over medium high heat. (A 14 inches or larger frying pan can be used. If you have neither use a Dutch oven.). Add oil and wait for 1 minute. Add chicken and brown until crispy on outside. Remove chicken from pan and set aside. Add sausage to pan and cook until nicely browned. Remove from pan and place with chicken. Add onions, garlic, and red pepper to pan and sauté until onions are translucent. Add herbs to pan and stir occasionally for 1 minute. Add rice to pan and continue to sauté for 3 minutes. Add 2 cups of stock to pan and bring to a boil.

Place chicken and sausage on top of rice. Reduce heat to medium. Continue to cook until liquid is almost absorbed/evaporated and add additional 2 cups stock. Continue to cook for 30 minutes, adding water in 2 cup increments as liquid continues to absorb and evaporate. Half way through cooking, turn chicken over once. After 30 minutes wait until liquid is absorbed again. Add shrimp and peas. Add last 2 cups of broth. Make sure shrimp get submerged in liquid. Bring to a boil and cook for 15 minutes. Test rice for doneness. If not done add more water and cycle again.

Whole Wheat Pasta with Fresh Tomato Meat Sauce

SERVES 6

1   pound whole wheat pasta
½   cup olive oil
2   tablespoons salt
2   pounds ground round or 88/12 blend
5   large tomatoes, cored and cut into large chunks
1   cup basil, chopped
2   tablespoons garlic clove, finely chopped
1   cup onions, finely chopped
½   cup carrots, peeled and thinly sliced
1   cup dry white wine
1   cup chicken stock, bouillon or broth
    grated parmesan cheese on the side

Bring large pot of water to a rapid boil. Add 2 table-spoons salt and 2 tablespoons olive oil to water. Add pasta noodles and cook until tender or al dente. Drain noodles in colander and toss with 2 tablespoons of olive oil.

In a large Dutch oven-style pan or pot add 2 table-spoons olive oil and heat on medium high. Add onions and carrots and sauté until onions are trans-lucent. Add beef and continue to cook until beef is thoroughly browned and liquids have mostly evapo-rated. Season lightly with salt and pepper.

Add tomatoes, basil, garlic and remaining olive oil. Continue cooking over medium heat for 15 minutes or until tomatoes have really broken down. Lightly season with salt and pepper. Add wine and stock. Bring to a boil. Reduce heat to low and cover. Cook for 30 minutes. Remove cover. If you prefer your sauce thicker, raise heat to medium high and reduce for an additional 10 minutes. Serve with grated parmesan cheese.

Southwest Braised Chicken
with Avocado Hummus

This dish marries together the tang and spice of homemade salsa with the juicy flavors of the chicken and an extra kick of zesty avocado hummus.

4   boneless skinless chicken breasts

2   tablespoons olive oil

1   medium diced onion

1   tablespoon diced garlic

1   tablespoon cumin

1   tablespoon fresh cilantro

1   teaspoon sea salt

½   teaspoon fresh ground black pepper

6   slices pickled jalapenos, diced

1   cup prepared mild salsa

½   cup chicken stock

2   cups of prepared Mexican/Spanish style rice
    (make with chicken stock if you have enough)

Heat olive oil in heavy bottom sauté pan. Season chicken breast with sea salt and pepper. Sear chicken breast on each side for a minute or so and remove from pan. Add onions to pan and sauté over medium heat for a couple of minutes. Add garlic jalapenos, cilantro and spices and continue to sauté for 2-3 minutes until onions are golden. In the sauté pan or transfer to a bowl, add chicken stock and prepared salsa. Mix until combined.

Place chicken breast in baking dish. Season with a sprinkle of sea salt and pepper. Pour salsa mixture over chicken and cover. Bake in a preheated 350 degree oven for 45 minutes, until chicken breast is cooked. Drain braising liquid into pot and reduce liquid by 30-40 percent (reserve ½ cup braising liquid). Divide rice evenly between 4 serving plates. Spoon a few tablespoons of braising liquid over the top of the rice, then set breast on top of rice and dollop with avocado hummus.

AVOCADO HUMMUS

Puree 1 avocado and 4 slices pickled jalapeno pepper in a food processor along with ½ cup of cooked white beans. Blend intermittingly with juice of two of limes. Finish with a sprinkle of sea salt and a pinch of cayenne. If bean mixture is too thick, add a couple tablespoons of water.

Chicken Marsala

5   6-8 ounce boneless and skinless chicken breasts

½   cup onions, finely chopped

2   tablespoons garlic clove, finely chopped

1   small sprig rosemary

4   sprigs thyme

1¼   cup chicken stock

¾   cup Marsala wine

4   tablespoons olive oil

½   pound button mushrooms, sliced

3   tablespoons butter

1   tablespoon arrowroot powder (optional)

3   tablespoons water (optional)

1   tablespoon Marsala wine for finishing sauce

Lightly brush chicken breasts with olive oil. Season liberally with salt and pepper. Preheat frying pan to medium high heat. Add 2 tablespoons olive oil and continue to heat for 1 minute. Add chicken breasts and sauté on both sides until nicely brown. Reduce heat to medium low and continue to cook for 10 minutes. Remove from pan and place on plate in a warm oven.

In same pan add mushrooms, onions, garlic, rosemary and thyme. Sauté on medium heat until onions are translucent and soft and mushrooms have some brown on edges. Season lightly with salt and pepper. Add Marsala wine and bring to a boil. Let wine reduce in half. Add chicken stock and bring to a boil. Let sauce reduce in half again. Reduce heat and slowly stir in butter.

At this point you can choose to thicken the sauce more if so desired. Stir arrowroot into water thoroughly. Add half of mixture to sauce and bring to boil while stirring. Add more if you want more thickness. Add chicken back into sauce and heat on simmer for 5 minutes. Prior to serving, splash sauce with an extra tablespoon of Marsala wine and stir. Place sauce on plate. Cut chicken in slices on a diagonal. Place on top of sauce. Garnish with extra rosemary sprig.

Chicken Mole Verde

2   chickens, cut into 8 pieces each

2   tablespoons salt

¼   cup olive oil

2   cups onion, finely chopped

2   tablespoons garlic clove, finely chopped

1   cup green bell pepper, seeded and chopped

2   tablespoons tomato paste

1   jar Mole Verde paste

4   cups chicken stock or canned chicken broth
    salt and pepper to taste

2   cups cooked white rice, held warm

1   package flour tortillas

Sprinkle salt all over chicken. Preheat a large Dutch oven-style pan on medium high heat. Place oil in pan and wait 1 minute. In batches, brown chicken thoroughly until crispy. Remove chicken from pan. Add onions, garlic, and green pepper to pan. Stirring occasionally, cook until translucent and you start to get some color on onions.

Create a small clearing in middle of pan with a spoon. Place tomato paste in this space and let cook until paste caramelizes on bottom of pan. Stir vegetables and paste together. Season lightly with salt and pepper. Open Mole Verde paste jar and pour off oil. Take rest of paste and add it to the vegetables. Stir until thoroughly incorporated. Add chicken stock and place chicken back in pan. Submerge chicken in sauce with spoon. Cover pan. Reduce heat to low. Let cook for 1 hour. Serve over white rice with flour tortillas.

Tacos Carnitas

The taste of the ever-so-slightly citrusy, well-seasoned pork makes any ordinary lunch or dinner a festive occasion.

4–6 pounds pork shoulder (pork butt) roast
    coarse salt
4 cups chicken stock, bouillon or broth
1 tablespoon curry powder
1 tablespoon ancho chile powder
1 tablespoon ground cumin
1 tablespoon ground allspice
1 large navel orange
1 package high quality corn tortillas
1 cup onions, finely chopped
1 cup cilantro, finely chopped
    vegetable oil to lightly coat pan
    salsa of your choice

In a very large pot or roasting pan, place pork roast and season generously with salt. Pour in stock, curry powder, allspice, cumin, and ancho chile powder. Slice orange in quarters. Squeeze juice into liquid and place rest of orange in the pot as well. Bring to a boil, cover and place in 350 degree oven for $3\frac{1}{2}-4$ hours until very tender to a fork. Remove from oven and open lid. With 2 forks shred pork and push down into liquid. Replace cover and set aside.

Heat a griddle to medium heat. (You can use a pan as well.) Lightly coat with oil. Heat tortillas until lightly browned on both sides. Top individual tortillas with pork, onions and cilantro. You can serve onions on the side if preferred. Serve with salsa of your choice.

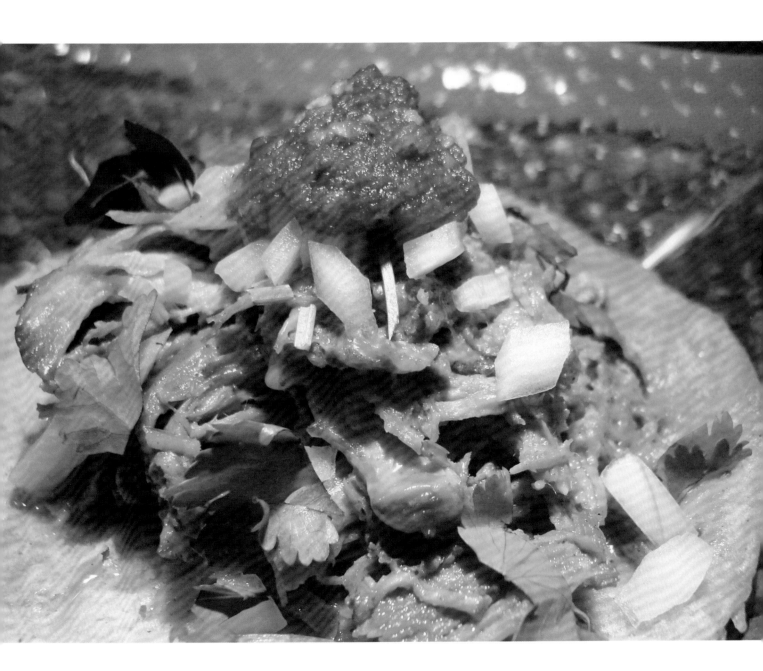

Beer Braised Short Ribs

SERVES 5

What goes better together than beer and ribs? Sink your teeth into this succulent, richly aromatic dish and you'll have your answer.

6   tablespoons olive oil

4   pounds boneless beef short ribs, trimmed of all fat

1   bottle beer

2   cups onion, chopped

1   tablespoon garlic clove, finely chopped

2   cups carrots, peeled and cut into ¾ inch slices

1   pound button mushrooms, cleaned and sliced in half

1   cup chicken stock, bouillon or broth

1   tablespoon Italian seasoning (or fresh rosemary and thyme)

¼   cup flour

1   cup water

    salt and pepper

Season beef thoroughly with salt and pepper. Preheat a large Dutch oven-style pot or pan over medium high heat for 5 minutes. Place 4 tablespoons of olive oil in pan for 30 seconds. In batches (do not crowd pan or meat will steam, not sear) sear meat until very crispy and brown on both cut sides. Remove from pot and set aside. Place onions and carrots in pan and cook until translucent. Season lightly with salt and pepper.

Add 2 tablespoons of olive oil, mushrooms and Italian seasonings (or three stems of thyme and one stem of rosemary) to pan. Cook until mushrooms have shrunk and are tender. Add beef back into pan. Add beer and stock. Bring pan to a boil and reduce to simmer. Cover and let cook for 2 hours.

Thoroughly stir water and flour together to form a slurry. Remove cover from pan. Increase heat to medium high and add slurry mixture. Bring mixture to a boil while gently stirring pot to let slurry slightly thicken the sauce. Turn off heat and taste for seasoning with salt and pepper.

Michigan Chicken Pasta Primavera

This colorful, healthy, classic recipe is a taste bud-enticing ode to my home state, Michigan.

2   quarts chicken stock

1   12-14 ounce box whole wheat pasta,
     bow tie or penne

     sea salt

     fresh ground pepper

1   head broccoli

2   tablespoons olive oil

1   medium onion, sliced thin

2-3 cloves garlic, minced

3   boneless, skinless chicken breasts cut into
     1 inch cubes

3   carrots, peeled and cut into thin strips

1   yellow pepper, cut into thin strips

1   red pepper, cut into thin strips

1   tablespoon dried Italian spices

½   cup dried cherries

½   cup slivered almonds, toasted

1   cup grated parmesan, divided

Bring chicken stock to a boil in a large pot and season with salt and pepper. Hold broccoli head from the stem in the boiling chicken stock. When broccoli turns bright green and has been cooked 30 seconds remove from stock and run under cold water. Cut off florets and reserve for the primavera. Add pasta to stock and cook according to package directions. Season chicken pieces with salt and pepper.

Meanwhile, add oil to a large sauté pan over medium heat and cook onion and garlic until fragrant and onion are translucent. Add chicken and sauté until cooked through. Add carrots, peppers and reserved broccoli, cooking until tender crisp. If need be add additional olive oil or chicken stock. Stir in dried cherries and almonds. Add Italian herbs and toss to coat. Drain pasta and reserve the chicken stock for another use, saving 1 cup. Toss pasta with chicken, vegetables and 1 cup of cooking liquid. Toss with ½ cup grated parmesan. Serve remaining parmesan on the side for garnish.

Oven Steamed Salmon and Vegetables

This ravishingly tasty entrée is not only pleasing to the eye but also to your health.

1½ pounds Wild King salmon skinned and
cut into 4 pieces (or whole fillet if desired)

1 cup of julienne carrots or packaged carrot shreds

1 cup fresh mushrooms, sliced

½ bunch of asparagus, cut in ½ inch pieces

1 small summer squash, cut julienne

1 bunch scallions, sliced

2 teaspoons fresh thyme, divided

2 cloves of minced garlic

½ cup chicken stock

sea salt and pepper

4 teaspoons olive oil

2 oranges, sliced thin

Butter a baking dish. Layer carrots, mushrooms, asparagus, squash, scallions, 1 teaspoon thyme and garlic in buttered dish. Season with a pinch of salt and pepper. Stir. Pour wine and chicken stock over vegetables. Season fish on both sides with salt and pepper. Top vegetable mixture with fish. Drizzle olive oil on top of the fish. Top with orange slices and additional thyme if desired. Bake covered at 350 degrees for about 20 minutes or until fish flakes easily with a fork. Serve with steamed brown rice or couscous.

Stuffed Grape Leaves

The grape leaves are stuffed with seasoned lamb and soak up all of the juicy goodness of the broth.

1   jar grape leaves, brined
1   pound ground lamb
1   cup rice
2   tablespoons tomato paste
½   cup onion, finely chopped
1   tablespoon garlic clove, finely chopped
1   teaspoon ground cumin
1   teaspoon ground allspice
1   tablespoon salt
1   teaspoon ground black pepper
2   cups carrots, sliced into ¼ inch rounds
2   cups chicken stock or canned chicken broth
2   tablespoons butter, cut into quarters

Place lamb, rice, salt, onions, garlic, tomato paste, cumin, and allspice together in a large bowl and mix together thoroughly. Place a large grape leaf on your counter or cutting board and place 3 tablespoons of meat mixture in the middle in a small log shape. Fold sides of grape leaf over ends of log and then roll the grape leaf over the middle of the log. Completely roll grape leaf over meat. Continue procedure with other grape leaves. If leaves are too small or broken, try stacking 2 on top of each other to get a good rolling surface.

Place carrots in the bottom of a large Dutch oven or deep frying pan. Carefully place the grape leaves on top of carrots and nestle together. Top with butter and pour over chicken stock. Bring to a boil on stove. Reduce to simmer and cover for 45 minutes. Remove cover and continue boiling until liquid is reduced in half. Remove grape leaves and serve with carrots on the side.

Middle Eastern Chicken Paprikash

1   4-5 pound chicken, cut into 8 pieces

¼   cup olive oil

1   cup onion, finely chopped

1   clove garlic clove, chopped

4   ounces button mushrooms, sliced

2   cups chicken stock or canned chicken broth

2   teaspoons dried oregano leaves

1   teaspoon sumac (optional)

2   tablespoons sweet paprika

½   cup Kefir cheese or sour cream

Salt and pepper chicken pieces aggressively. In a large Dutch oven-style pan or pot heat oil over medium high heat for 3 minutes. Add chicken and brown thoroughly on all sides. Remove from pan. Add onions, garlic, oregano, sumac and paprika to pan and sauté until onions are translucent. Add mushrooms and continue to sauté until mushrooms are soft. Add chicken back to pan and add stock. Reduce heat to medium. Cover and cook for 30 minutes. Turn chicken over once during this time. Remove lid and stir in Kafır or sour cream. Continue to cook with lid off for 10 minutes. Can be served over pasta or rice.

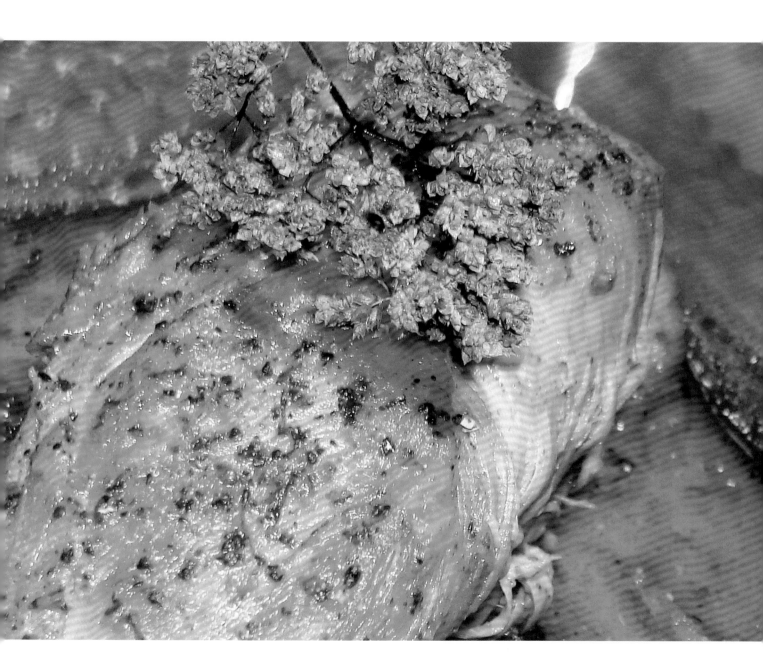

Tropical Pulled Pork Salad SERVES 6

5–6 pounds pork shoulder (pork butt) roast

2 tablespoons coarse salt

ROASTING LIQUID

3 cups chicken stock or canned chicken broth

1 cup rice wine vinegar

1 jalapeno pepper, whole

1 habanero pepper, whole

1 teaspoon hot curry powder

1 cup onion, chopped

2 tablespoons garlic clove, chopped

BARBECUE SAUCE

1 cup brown sugar

¼ cup Worcestershire sauce

¼ cup soy sauce

¼ cup Meyer's rum

1 teaspoon dry mustard

2 tablespoons Thai garlic chili sauce

1 cup ketchup

½ teaspoon black pepper

SALAD

1 pineapple, peeled, cut into rings and cored

1 large Bibb lettuce

1 large red Bibb lettuce

¼ cup olive oil

2 tablespoons fresh lemon juice

salt and pepper to taste

Rub pork roast with coarse salt. Place in very large Dutch oven. In a bowl, whisk together chicken stock, vinegar, peppers, curry, onions and garlic. Pour over meat. Cover and place in 350 degree oven. Bake for 4½ hours. Remove from oven. Put pork on a cutting board. With 2 large forks, pull pork into small strips.

In a large saucepan, whisk together soy sauce, Worcestershire sauce, Meyer's rum, brown sugar, dry mustard, garlic chili paste, ketchup and pepper. Bring to a boil over medium heat. Reduce heat to low and cook for 10 minutes. Add pulled pork to sauce and cook for an additional 10 minutes.

Toss salad with lemon juice and olive oil. Season lightly with salt and pepper. Mound salad portions on plate.

Preheat grill or grill pan over medium high heat. Lightly season pineapple with salt and pepper. If using grill pan, lightly coat with non-stick spray. Grill pineapple slices until nice brown marks are evident. Remove from heat and place on plate. Mound portions of salad on cold plates. Top with generous portion of pulled pork and top with a pine-apple slice.

Five-Star Fare

How hard is it to replicate the fine dining experience you have in a restaurant at home? Not that hard, actually. When you know how to make really good broth, many of your dishes will already have an edge in the taste department.

Just the very sound of these exceptionally luscious-tasting recipes—Frenched Double Pork Chops with Vidalia Dijon Cream Sauce, Chicken and Artichoke Murat, "Barber" Pork Loin with Pumpkin Polenta—will have you getting down to serious business in the kitchen. No James Beard-level skills are necessary here, however—just let the succulent, brothy juices do their work. But before we get too refined, we bring it back home-style with recipes like Johnny Prep's Restaurant Style Mac and Cheese, Savory Citrus Chicken, and many more recipes that taste as if they were crafted in Spago's kitchen.

The best part of creating these five-star dishes at home? No reservations are required.

Frenched Double Pork Chops with Vidalia Dijon Cream Sauce

SERVES 4

The epitome of five-star fare shines through in this lusciously moist pork chop dish, with the caramelized onions complimenting the tender tanginess of the Dijon mustard.

1 tablespoon olive oil

4 double cut pork chops

½ teaspoon garlic powder

½ teaspoon onion powder

½ teaspoon sweet paprika

1 teaspoon salt

½ teaspoon black pepper

DIJON VIDALIA CREAM SAUCE

1 large onion, cut into strips

1 tablespoon Dijon mustard

1 tablespoon olive oil

1 cup chicken stock or bouillon

¼ cup cream

  salt and pepper

  chopped parsley for garnish

French each chop by scraping all the meat and fat from each bone down to the loin. Place chops in a brine solution of salted water with equal amounts of sugar. Let brine for 1 hour. Remove and thoroughly pat dry with a paper towel. Preheat oven to 350 degrees. Brush chops lightly with olive oil.

Mix seasoning in a bowl. Sprinkle seasoning mixture aggressively on chops to coat evenly. Preheat grill or grill pan on medium high heat. Sear chops until nice grill marks are evident and meat is browned. Remove chops and place in a foil lined baking pan. Place in oven and bake for 20 minutes. Remove from oven. Tent with foil and let rest for at least 5 minutes.

While chops are baking, preheat a frying pan to medium heat. Add olive oil to pan and heat for 1 minute. Add onions to pan and sauté until onions are soft and translucent with a touch of brown color. Add mustard to pan and toss onions to coat. Continue cooking for 2 minutes. Add chicken stock. Bring to a boil and reduce for 3 minutes. Add cream and let reduce for an additional 2 minutes or until you reach desired sauce thickness. Season with salt and pepper to taste.

Spoon sauce on a plate and place 1 pork chop in the middle. Garnish with chopped parsley.

"Barber" Pork Loin with Pumpkin Polenta SERVES 6

The flavors of the harvest are all here, along with some satisfyingly complimentary ingredients—sage, pumpkin, cinnamon, and Parmesan coupled with prosciutto-wrapped pork loin.

½ whole pork loin, brined or fresh (3-4 pounds)
2 tablespoons unsalted butter
20 sage leaves
8–10 slices of prosciutto
½ cup chicken stock

Season pork with sea salt and pepper. Place prosciutto on clean work surface in overlapping rows. Place sage leaves intermittingly on prosciutto. Place pork in center and roll. Temper in freezer for 30 minutes.

Sear wrapped pork loin on hot flat surface with a tablespoon for olive oil. Brown on all sides. Transfer pork to ovenproof dish. Add chicken stock and cover. Finish is 350 degree oven for 20 minutes or until temperature reads 135-140. Let rest, then slice half inch slices and serve on platter with pumpkin polenta.

PUMPKIN POLENTA

3½ cups chicken stock
1 cup white grits/cornmeal
⅓ cup heavy cream
½ cup fresh shaved Parmesan cheese
1½ teaspoons sea salt
1 teaspoon fresh cracked black pepper
½ teaspoon cinnamon
1 cup pumpkin puree
3 tablespoons shaved Parmesan cheese
½ cup ricotta cheese
2 tablespoons chopped sage
2 tablespoons olive oil for drizzle

In heavy bottom rondo-style pan, bring chicken stock or water to a simmer and add grits in a very slow stream, whisking until completely incorporated. Add seasoning. Continue to stir with wooden spoon, stirring often over low heat until all the liquid is absorbed and the polenta is thick and soft, about 20 minutes. Add pumpkin puree and continue to cook another 5 or so minutes. Add cream and Parmesan cheese and simmer for an additional minute until all is combined well. Stir in sage and mound onto platter in big spoonfuls and arrange Barber-style pork next to pumpkin polenta. Spoon ricotta cheese over polenta peaks and sprinkle with parmesan cheese, sage and a drizzle of olive oil.

Steamed Snapper with
Black Bean Garlic Sauce SERVES 4

The steamed snapper is immersed in the savory essence of the black bean sauce, while the seafood stock just adds another layer of juicy flavor.

1	2-3 pounds whole yellow tail snapper, scales removed
1½	cups seafood stock (chicken stock can be substituted)
¼	cup ginger root, in large slivers
4	scallions cut in 3 pieces (use green part as well)
1½	cups cilantro sprigs (reserve some for garnish)
½	cup Asian black bean sauce
	salt and pepper
2	cloves garlic, slivered

Lightly season fish with salt and pepper. In a fish steamer or large broad pot with steamer, place stock and black bean sauce. Stir to incorporate. Cut 4-5 slits on a diagonal into flesh of skin and place fish in pot. Place 1 cup cilantro, ginger, scallions and garlic on fish. Place on high heat and bring to a boil. Reduce heat to medium. Cover and cook for 15 minutes or until fish is tender to a fork.

Remove fish. Pull off skin with a fork, then pull fish off bones with a fork. Serve in bowls. Pour steaming broth over fish and garnish with cilantro sprigs.

Asian Noodle Salad with Thai Peanut Sauce

SERVES 5

Flavorsome vegetarian dish with a ton of color and nutrients!

1	pound angel hair pasta
2	tablespoons vegetable oil
1	cup bean sprouts
½	cup chopped cilantro
2	tablespoons sesame oil
1	cup julienned red pepper
1	cup julienned carrot
1	cup julienned cucumber
½	cup thinly sliced green onion
1½	tablespoons minced ginger root
1	tablespoon Chinese chili and garlic paste
1	tablespoon minced garlic
1	tablespoon minced green onions
½	cup crunchy peanut butter
2	tablespoons soy sauce
¼	cup sherry vinegar
1	teaspoon sugar
2	tablespoons vegetable oil
1	teaspoon hot, dry mustard
½	teaspoon salt
½	cup vegetable or chicken stock
	salad or kale leaves for garnish

Boil pasta in a large pot of salted water until tender. Drain and rinse thoroughly in cold water until noodles are cool. Toss gently with vegetable oil and set aside. In a bowl, whisk together ginger root, garlic, minced green onions, peanut butter, soy sauce, vinegar, chili paste, sugar, 1 tablespoon of the sesame oil, vegetable oil, dry mustard, salt and stock. Whisk thoroughly until peanut butter is completely integrated into a smooth sauce. Set sauce aside.

Toss bean sprouts, pasta, cilantro and the rest of the sesame oil in a bowl. Place salad or kale leaves around perimeter of serving platter. Loosely pile pasta in center of leaves, leaving leaf edges to frame the dish. Drizzle on a healthy sprinkling of peanut sauce. Arrange vegetables in layers on top of pasta so that the colors are well blended. Lightly sprinkle again with peanut sauce and garnish lightly with thinly sliced green onions (or cilantro if you're not fond of too much raw onion).

Udon Noodles with Red Lentils, Peanuts, and Thai Curry Sauce SERVES 4

8 ounces thin organic Udon noodles

1 tablespoon sesame oil

½ cup red lentils

1 cup peanuts, chopped

½ cup cilantro, finely chopped

¼ cup mint, finely chopped

2 tablespoons vegetable oil

2 tablespoons red curry paste

½ cup Thai coconut milk

½ cup chicken stock or bouillon

Place lentils in a bowl and cover with boiling water (water from an instant hot tap works well) and let soften for 2 hours. If not soft add more hot water and continue to soak for another half hour. You can also just cover with hot water overnight. Bring large pot of salted water to a boil. Place noodles in water and boil until tender. Drain and toss with sesame oil.

In a large frying pan, place oil over medium high heat. Stir in red curry paste and cook for 2-3 minutes. Stir in coconut milk and chicken stock and mix until paste is thoroughly incorporated. Add half the cilantro and mint and reduce sauce by ⅓. Place drained noodles in sauce along with half of the peanuts and half of the lentils. Toss to coat noodles and cook for 3 minutes. Plate noodles with rest of peanuts, lentils and cilantro. Place mint on top as garnish.

Chicken and Artichoke Murat SERVES 6

The crusty sautéed chicken contrasted against the smooth, nutritious flavors of the vegetables in this dish will make your taste buds pop!

3   eggs, beaten

2   cups fresh bread crumbs

6   4-6 ounce chicken breasts, boned and skinned

1   cup olive oil, for frying

4   large artichoke bottoms, rough chopped

2   large Roma tomatoes, rough chopped

4   ounces button mushrooms, halved

1   tablespoon garlic clove, chopped
    pinch cayenne pepper (optional)

¼   cup chicken stock or bouillon

1   large lemon

½   cup parsley, chopped fine

2   tablespoons butter
    salt and pepper

Set up bread crumbs and eggs in separate dredging bowls. Lightly salt and pepper each chicken breast. Dredge each breast in eggs and then bread crumbs, applying pressure with your hands on bread crumbs. Preheat large frying pan on medium high heat with ¾ cup olive oil in it to sauté the chicken. Place chicken breasts in pan. Reduce heat to medium. Do not crowd; you can do this in batches and keep the done ones warm in the oven while doing the second batch.

Sauté until nicely deep brown on both sides and chicken is done (about 7 minutes per side). Remove from pan and place on a paper towel. Lightly season with salt and place in a warm oven while making murat.

In a large sauté pan preheat ¼ cup oil on medium high heat. Place mushrooms in pan then lightly salt and pepper. Sauté mushrooms until they are soft and show some color. Add artichoke bottoms and continue to cook for 3 minutes. Add tomatoes, cayenne pepper and garlic and cook for another 3 minutes. Stir occasionally throughout this process. Season again lightly with salt and pepper. Reduce heat to medium and squeeze the juice from half your lemon into the pan. Stir and cook for 2 minutes. Add the chicken stock. Stir slightly and cook for another 2 minutes.

Add parsley to pan and stir. Add butter to pan in 3 chunks and stir to melt butter. Season with salt and pepper to taste. Slice chicken breasts on a bias and serve over vegetables. Garnish with parsley. Cut second half of lemon into wedges and squeeze lemon juice from one wedge on each serving before eating.

Savory Citrus Chicken SERVES 5

1 whole chicken, cut into 10 pieces
2 tablespoons olive oil
1 cup onion, finely chopped
2 cloves garlic, finely chopped
2 cups chicken stock, bouillon or broth
1 large navel orange
1 lemon
½ cup cilantro, finely chopped
  salt and pepper

Preheat large frying pan on medium high. Season chicken pieces generously with salt and pepper. Add oil to pan and let heat for 30 seconds. Add chicken to pan. Brown chicken thoroughly until crispy on both sides. Reduce heat to medium. Add onions and garlic. Sauté until onions are translucent, stirring occasionally (about 5 minutes).

Using a zesting tool, peel lemon and orange strips for use as a garnish. Cut both orange and lime in half and squeeze juice through a strainer into pan. It helps to get more juice out of the citrus if you roll the fruit on the counter under the pressure of your hand before you cut it in half. Add chicken broth. Bring to a boil and then reduce to simmer. Cover pan and let simmer for 30 minutes. Remove cover and increase heat to medium to reduce sauce. Continue cooking for 15 more minutes or until meat is done and almost falling off the bone. Plate chicken, pour sauce over it, and garnish with zest.

Chicken Piccata

¼ cup olive oil

1 whole chicken, cut into 10 pieces

1 cup onion, finely chopped

2 tablespoons garlic clove, finely chopped

¼ cup capers, drained

¼ cup lemon juice, freshly squeezed

1 cup dry white wine of your choice

1 cup chicken stock or bouillon

¼ cup parsley, minced

4 tablespoons butter (optional)

Preheat olive oil in a large frying pan over medium high heat (don't let smoke). Season chicken aggressively with salt and pepper. Place chicken in hot oil and brown thoroughly on both sides turning once. Reduce heat to medium. Add onions, garlic and capers to pan. Cook until onions are soft and translucent. Add lemon juice and cook 2 more minutes. Add wine and chicken stock and simmer for another 30 minutes. Add parsley and cook for 5 more minutes. Season sauce with salt and pepper to taste. If you desire to thicken with butter, add 1 tablespoon at a time and whisk it in by hand.

Johnny Prep's Restaurant Style Mac and Cheese

SERVES 8

2 tablespoons olive oil

1 cup onions, finely chopped

½ cup carrots, grated

½ cup celery, finely chopped

1 clove garlic clove, crushed and finely chopped

1 teaspoon fresh thyme, (or ½ dry)

1 bay leaf

1 teaspoon Old Bay seasoning

2 cups ham, small dice

2 tablespoons butter

3 tablespoons flour

2 cups rich chicken broth

1 cup heavy whipping cream

12 ounces white cheddar cheese, grated

12 ounces Colby cheese, grated

1 pound large elbow macaroni noodles, cooked al dente

1 pound lump crab meat, optional (can also substitute cooked shrimp or lobster)

salt and fresh ground pepper to taste

1 cup Panko bread crumbs

1 teaspoon Italian seasoning

1 tablespoon olive oil

In a large Dutch oven-style pan, heat 2 tablespoons olive oil over medium high heat. Add ham and sauté until ham has browned nicely and there is brown (fond) on the bottom of the pan. Stir occasionally. Add onions, carrots, celery, thyme, bay leaf, garlic and Old Bay seasoning and sauté until onions are opaque and tender. Season lightly with salt and pepper. Reduce the heat to medium. Add butter and flour and stir gently for 3 minutes. Add chicken stock and bring to a boil, stirring gently. Add cream and stir to incorporate. Add both cheeses in four batches and stir to incorporate and melt. Stir cooked macaroni noodles into sauce and turn off heat. Gently fold in optional crab meat. Season to taste with salt and pepper.

In a small bowl toss 1 tablespoon olive oil, Panko bread crumbs and Italian seasoning. Spread macaroni into a large buttered casserole or baking dish. Sprinkle bread crumb mixture evenly on top of macaroni. Bake in a 400 degree oven for 30 minutes or until bread crumbs are nicely browned.

Pan Grilled Chicken Gremolata

This savory, multi-dimensionally flavored, foolproof entrée will have your guests praising your kitchen mastery!

CHICKEN

4	boneless, skin-on chicken breast halves, tenderloins removed, 5-6 ounces
1	tablespoon extra-virgin olive oil
	sea salt and fresh ground black pepper
½	cup chicken stock
¼	cup white wine

PARMESAN GREMOLATA

1	small clove garlic
¼	teaspoon sea salt
1	lemon, zest finely minced
¼	cup minced flat-leaf parsley
2	tablespoons extra-virgin olive oil
4	tablespoons good quality grated Parmesan
1	tablespoon Dijon mustard
¼	teaspoon sea salt and sprinkle of pepper

Mix all of the Parmesan Gremolata ingredients in small bowl.

Heat a sauté pan over medium high heat. Preheat broiler on low. Heat olive oil in sauté pan. Season raw breast meat before cooking with salt, pepper and olive oil. Place the seasoned chicken in pan skin side down and cook 3-4 minutes, then flip to back side and deglaze with chicken stock and white wine. Cover and cook over medium heat for 3-4 more minutes until chicken breast is firm to touch and cooked through. Place chicken in baking dish or use pan you grilled chicken in if it is oven-proof. Divide the Gremolata evenly over breasts and gently press mixture down on to top of breast. Broil on low for 2-4 minutes until golden brown and crispy.

Moroccan Chicken Bake

SERVES 4-6

The chicken is the star player here, with a huge assist from the unique, diverse combination of herbs and seasonings and the sweet, earthly flavors of fig, onion, tomato, and quinoa.

1	roaster chicken, about 5 to 6 pounds cut into 8 pieces
2	cloves garlic, minced
1	branch fresh rosemary, leaves removed and minced
	sea salt and pepper
3–4	tablespoons extra-virgin olive oil
2	yellow onions, diced
¾	cup sliced dried figs
½	cup white wine
1	14 ounce can diced tomatoes
1½	cups chicken stock
1	cup quinoa, rinsed
2	tablespoons brown sugar
1½	teaspoons allspice
1¼	teaspoons cumin
	pinch red chili flakes (reserve for baking)
1	tablespoon fresh chopped parsley for garnish (optional)

Combine the garlic, rosemary, sugar, allspice, cumin salt, pepper and enough olive oil to make a somewhat dry paste. Generously season cut up chicken pieces. Divide the paste evenly among the 8 pieces and let sit, covered, and refrigerated for 2 hours.

In a Dutch oven, heat 3 tablespoons olive oil over high heat until smoking. Brush the excess rub from the bird and sear each piece of meat on all sides in the hot oil. Add the onions and cook over medium heat until onions are golden brown. Stir in sliced figs, lemon juice, chicken stock, red pepper seeds, and diced tomatoes and then stir the bottom of the pan with a wooden spoon to dislodge the browned bits. Add cup of rinsed quinoa into pot with liquid, then place chicken back in pot on top of liquid and bake covered for 25 minutes.

Remove lid and bake an additional 20 minutes until chicken is cooked through. Remove chicken from pot and set aside. Divide quinoa onto four plates and top with chicken as desired. Drizzle extra braising liquid from pot over entrées and sprinkle with herbs.

Stuffed Turkey Breast Roulade SERVES 6-8

While many equate turkey and cranberry with Thanksgiving, this mouth-wateringly fruited plate is truly destined to become a year-round favorite in your home.

BRINE (OPTIONAL)

½   cup kosher salt

½   cup light brown sugar

1   gallon water

1   tablespoon black peppercorns

1   teaspoon allspice berries

Combine all ingredients and add meat. Use a weight to keep meat submerged in brine. Refrigerate overnight.

TURKEY

1   boneless turkey breast (about 4 pounds), brined overnight (optional, adds moisture), trimmed and butterflied, season with sea salt and pepper

1   cup chicken stock

3   tablespoons butter or olive oil mixed with

3   tablespoons chopped herbs (to rub on top of flesh before covering with skin)

Dried Cranberry Cornbread Stuffing (see recipe on page 160)

VEGETABLE RACK

2   carrots

1   green apple

1   small onion

3   celery stalks

GLAZE

½   cup apple cider

3   tablespoons real maple syrup

1   tablespoon chipotle pepper puree

Preheat oven to 375 degrees. Remove turkey from brine. Remove skin from turkey and reserve. Place turkey breast skinned side down on a cutting board. Spread halves of breast apart so breast opens like a book. Release tenders (strips of meat) from breast. With a sharp knife, slice through thickest part of each breast half, creating flaps that you can open to create a more uniform thickness. Cover turkey with plastic wrap. Gently pound with mallet or small heavy pot to an even thickness (about ¾ inch thick). Remove plastic. Season with salt and pepper.

Spread stuffing over surface of breast in an even layer. Tightly roll turkey breast, starting from your left side, to enclose stuffing. Rub herb butter or olive

oil mixture on top of breast. Center reserved skin over top of roast and wrap turkey tightly, smoothing skin out over meat to remove any air pockets beneath skin. Using a few short lengths of kitchen twine, tie roast at 3 or 4 evenly spaced intervals to keep skin from coming loose. Rub oil over skin, and season generously with salt and pepper. Place vegetable rack on a roasting pan. Transfer turkey seam side down into roasting pan on top of vegetables. Add chicken stock and cover. Roast for 30 minutes covered with lid or foil.

Meanwhile prepare the glaze. Combine all ingredients in a small pan over medium low heat. Reduce for 5 minutes or volume by half. Glaze turkey after 25 minutes of roasting and re-baste every 5-8 minutes until turkey is cooked. Turkey is done when a probe thermometer inserted in the thickest part reads 160 degrees. After another 20 or so minutes cover turkey breast again with foil if breast is browning too much and is not cooked through. Let turkey rest for 10 minutes before slicing.

3	tablespoons olive oil or butter
1	small onion, diced small
2	ribs celery, diced small
1	large Granny Smith apple, diced medium
2	teaspoons sea salt
1	teaspoon fresh ground pepper
3	cloves garlic, minced
½	cup coarsely chopped walnuts
3	cups stale cornbread, cut into 1-inch cubes (about 12 muffins)
1	cup fresh spinach
½	cup dried cranberries
1½	cups chicken stock

Coat a large sauté pan with olive oil. Add the onions, celery and apples. Sauté over medium heat. Season with salt and pepper. Cook until the vegetables start to become soft and are very aromatic. Stir in the garlic and sauté for another 1 to 2 minutes. Add cherries, spinach and walnuts. Cook for another minute. Remove from heat and let cool. In a large bowl mix together the cornbread, cranberries, and chicken stock and knead with your hands or stir with spoon until the bread is very moist, actually wet. (Add a little more stock if it seems too dry.) Check for seasoning and season with additional sea salt and pepper if needed. Transfer to an ovenproof dish or use as a filling in turkey roulade. If baking separately, bake the stuffing until it is hot all the way through and is crusty on top, about 25 to 30 minutes.

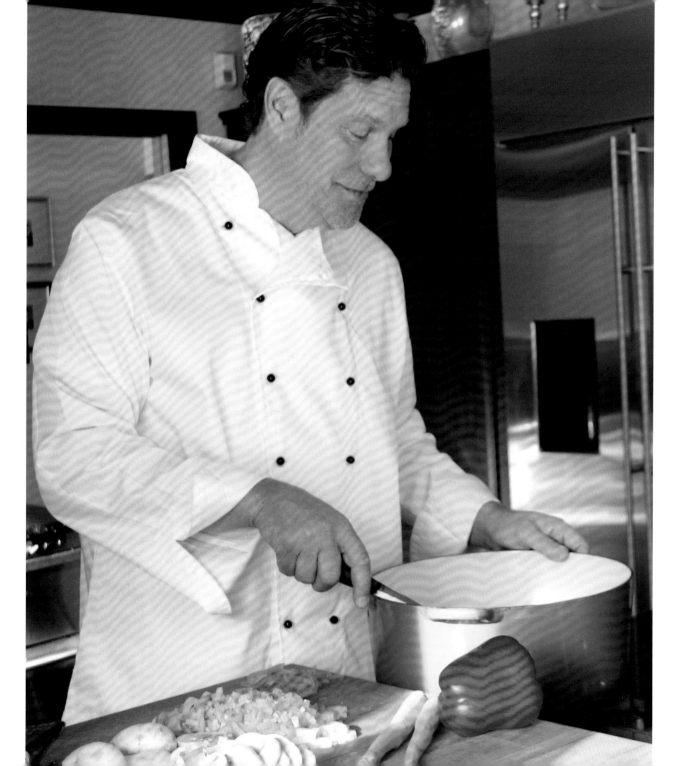

Bouillabaisse

½   cup olive oil

2   cups onions, finely chopped

2   cups fennel bulbs (white part), finely chopped

1   teaspoon hot pepper flakes

2   tablespoons garlic clove, finely chopped

4   cups tomatoes, diced

½   cup fresh basil, chopped

4   cups seafood stock (chicken stock can be substituted)

1   cup white wine

½   teaspoon saffron

2   pounds 21–25 count shrimp, peeled and deviened

1   pound sea scallops, tough part of muscle removed

2   pounds mussels, debearded

    salt and pepper to taste

    garlic bread

Place olive oil in large Dutch oven shaped pan and preheat over medium heat for 3 minutes. Place onions, fennel, pepper flakes and garlic in pan and sweat vegetables until onion and fennel are soft and translucent. Season lightly with salt and pepper. Add tomatoes and basil, and continue to cook until tomatoes start breaking down into a sauce. Add wine, stock and saffron. Bring to a boil over high heat and reduce to a simmer. Let simmer for 30 minutes.

Place scallops and shrimp in broth and bring to a boil over high heat. Reduce heat to medium and let cook for 5 minutes. Add mussels and continue to cook for another 3 minutes or until mussels have opened. Serve in a bowl with garlic bread as a garnish.

Cioppino

4	ounces bacon, diced
2	cups onions, chopped
1	cup fennel bulbs (white part), finely chopped
2	cups corn, cut off the cob
2	tablespoons garlic clove, crushed and finely chopped
¼	cup olive oil
5	large tomatoes, chopped into small pieces
6	cups seafood stock (chicken stock can be substituted)
1	teaspoon red pepper flakes
¾	cup basil, chopped
2	pounds shrimp, 31-40 count, peeled and de-veined
1	pound sea scallops, halved with tough part of muscle removed
1	pound lump crab meat
1	pounds mussels, debearded (optional)

In a large Dutch oven style pan render bacon until crispy over medium heat. Remove bacon, drain on paper towel, and set aside.

Discard half of the fat. Add onion, fennel, corn, and garlic. Season lightly with salt and pepper. Cook until vegetables are soft and browned. (Be patient, you may have to turn heat to medium low.) Scrape bottom of pan frequently to remove caramelized starch from corn. Keep doing this; it develops the sweetness of the corn. Add basil, tomatoes, red pepper flakes, and olive oil to the pan. Season again lightly with salt and pepper. Cook for 15 minutes on medium heat or until tomatoes have broken down into a sauce. Add seafood stock and continue to cook for 10 minutes. Add seafood and bacon to the pan. Bring to a simmer and cook for 10 more minutes. Season with salt and pepper to taste. Serve with croutons or garlic bread.

Acknowledgements

The success of any publishing endeavor requires the nuanced talents and unwavering dedication of a collaborative, creative team. And I have been especially blessed to have had the opportunity to work with an extremely gifted group of people to produce *The Magic of Cooking with Really Good Broth*.

I first met Chef Kelli Lewton, who contributed about one-fifth of the recipes to this project, at Schoolcraft College Culinary School in metro Detroit. She was my instructor for a breakfast, salads, and sandwich class. With mastery and enthusiasm, she taught us the finer points of making French omelets, crepes, and many other egg skills. We struck up a lasting friendship that has turned into a culinary partnership.

Kelli and I team up on a number of projects, especially those focused on healthy eating and working with kids. Kelli is profoundly dedicated to locally produced, wholesome foods and is a proprietor of Pure Food 2U (www.purefood2u.com), a delivery service that provides gourmet meals made primarily from locally sourced, organic products. As a caterer and event planner, Kelli also owns 2 Unique Catering (www.twounique.com), a southeast Michigan mainstay for high-end catered foods.

I have also had the great pleasure of working with Jennifer Pullinger, a Virginia-based writer and editor, who helped shape the cookbook's text. As a person who likes to write but has many grammatical and structural deficiencies, I have found Jennifer's support to be fantastic. Her experience in writing and publishing has elevated the quality of this cookbook immeasurably.

I also want to extend my thanks to Nancy Freeborn, who has applied her artistic craft to the cookbook's design. Supplementing my photos, I must thank Sandy Topping from SweetEye Photography who expertly contributed a number of images, helping to make this a truly visually appealing cookbook.

This cookbook and its associated media are the beneficiaries of the knowledge and skills bestowed upon me by Chefs Shawn Loving, CEC and Chef Jeffrey Gabriel, CMC. Both are inspirational teachers and world-class chefs.

Most importantly, I want to acknowledge and thank my family for their encouragement. My beautiful and loving wife Sara has shown endless support throughout my adventurous career. My children Joe, Jesse, and Jackson keep me on top of my game every day in the kitchen. And a big, big thanks to my mother Lucy, who was there in the beginning to teach, nurture, and inspire my culinary aspirations.

About the Author

Chef Johnny Prep is an author, entrepreneur, cooking show host, soup expert, and an advocate for children's health. The author of *The Five-Star Entertaining Casual Cookbook* published in 2012, he now hosts "Soup and Co." airing in the Detroit metro area. He is the founder of "Veggie Wars," an innovative middle school curriculum developed through his Quality for Kids nonprofit, and a culinary partner with Zoup! Fresh Soup Company. Johnny lives in Bloomfield Hills, Detroit with his wife Sarah and three kids, Jackson, Jesse, and Joe. Find him online at www.johnnyprep.com.

Index